The Checklist to End Tyranny

*HOW DISSIDENTS
WILL WIN
21ST CENTURY
CIVIL RESISTANCE
CAMPAIGNS*

PETER ACKERMAN

ICNC PRESS

The Checklist to End Tyranny: How Dissidents
Will Win 21st Century Civil Resistance Campaigns

by Peter Ackerman
First edition: September 2021
Published by ICNC Press

International Center on Nonviolent Conflict

600 New Hampshire Ave NW, Suite 710
Washington, D.C. 20037 USA

www.nonviolent-conflict.org
CONTACT: icnc@nonviolent-conflict.org

ISBN: 978-1-943271-50-4

The Checklist to End Tyranny

*Photo: Early stages of the
Jasmine Revolution that unseated
President Ben Ali in Tunisia, 2010.*

Acknowledgments

FOLLOWING GENE SHARP'S passing in 2018, there is only one person who has been with me on this journey from the beginning. That is Joanne Leedom-Ackerman, my wife of 49 years. Through all this time she has been emphatic about why advancing understanding of nonviolent conflict is critical to preserving human rights and democratic governance—values we have always shared.

In addition to Joanne's vital encouragement, this book would not have been written without Hardy Merriman, the President and CEO of the International Center on Nonviolent Conflict. An earlier version of the Checklist can be found in a chapter I co-authored with Hardy for an edited volume published by the Atlantic Council, *Is Authoritarianism Staging a Comeback?* His thought partnership and contributions are reflected at various points in this book, and he has been diligent in bringing *The Checklist to End Tyranny* to publication by ICNC Press. Special thanks has to go to Maciej Bartkowski, Bruce Pearson, Alice Wren, and Lillian Hathaway for editing many drafts.

I am indebted to many scholars whose work was referenced in the book and who have offered critical advice. They include Maria Stephan, Erica Chenoweth, Stephen Zunes, Jonathan Pinckney, and Ivan Marovic.

Others who have reviewed the text include Aaron Lobel, Reuben Brigety, and Hans Binnendijk.

In the aggregate they have sharpened ideas and identified contradictions and important omissions. This volume has been significantly improved by their input.

At left: The No Campaign opposing Augusto Pinochet in Chile, 1988.

It is generally assumed that tyrannies persist because they possess a monopoly on the use of force. *Yet oppressed populations using nonviolent tactics—such as strikes, boycotts, and mass protests—are often the most powerful drivers of their own liberation.*

Chapter One

1

INTRODUCTION:

The Evolving Role of Civil Resistance in the Battle Against Tyranny

I t is generally assumed that tyrannies persist because they possess a monopoly on the use of force. While violence against their citizens can be decisive for a time, there is a better explanation: Tyrannies persist as long as citizens fail to understand how—without needing to resort to violence—they can undermine the tyrant's base of support and force him from power. Oppressed populations using nonviolent tactics—such as strikes, boycotts, mass protests, and other forms of disrupting societal order—are often the most powerful drivers of their own liberation.

Increasingly this good news has been embraced by dissidents and others concerned with the advancement of human rights and democratic governance free from corruption. Yet the potential of civil resistance remains widely underrecognized because its premises sharply challenge conventional assumptions about the nature of power. Policymakers, scholars, journalists, and other interested observers consistently overestimate the extent to which tyrants can rely on violence to manipulate a population they assume they control. At the same time, they underestimate the capacity of ordinary people to undermine tyranny and achieve rights through the strategic use of nonviolent tactics.

These insights came to me a half a century ago. Since then, I have endeavored to transmit this knowledge to dissidents and pro-democracy activists so they can realize their unlimited opportunities to live in freer societies.

In the early to mid-1970s I was a PhD candidate in Strategic Studies at the Fletcher School of Law and Diplomacy at Tufts University. The failure of US military forces in Vietnam prompted my interest in asymmetric warfare. This involved studying how adversaries with significantly inferior military capabilities can wage conflict by utilizing highly differentiated strategies and tactics involving economic, cultural, and psychological factors. One of my courses on strategic theory was taught by Harvard Professor Thomas Schelling, who went on to win the 2005 Nobel Prize in Economic Sciences. Schelling was considered the preeminent scholar on how to communicate intent between the United States and the Soviet Union in order to reduce the threat of accidental nuclear war.

I approached Professor Schelling after a lecture to discuss how protagonists with inferior military capabilities could prevail in conflicts against adversaries with superior military capabilities. He responded with a challenge: If you are interested in studying why protagonists with inferior military resources could prevail, then why not instead explore how protagonists with no military resources at all could succeed?

Professor Schelling introduced me to Gene Sharp, who was about to publish his iconic three-volume study, *The Politics of Nonviolent Action*. At the center of Sharp's thinking was a thesis about power which harkened back to the centuries-old work of Étienne de La Boétie in his *Discourse on Voluntary Servitude*, published in 1576. De La Boétie wrote:

> *Resolve to serve no more, and you are at once freed. I do not ask that you place hands upon the tyrant to topple him over, but simply that you support him no longer; then you will behold him, like a great Colossus whose pedestal has been pulled away, fall of his own weight and break in pieces.*[1]

---

1   Etienne de La Boétie, "Discours de la Servitude Volontaire," Oeuvres Complètes d'Etienne de La Boétie (Paris: J. Rouam & Cie, 1892): 12–14, quoted in Gene Sharp, *The Politics of Nonviolent Action, Part One: Power and Struggle* (Boston, MA: Porter Sargent Publishers, 1973), 34.

Here is Sharp's contemporary version of this insight:

> *In political terms, nonviolent action is based on a very simple postulate: people do not always do what they are told to do, and sometimes they act in ways that have been forbidden to them. Subjects may disobey laws they reject. Workers may halt work, which may paralyze the economy. The bureaucracy may refuse to carry out instructions. Soldiers and police may become lax in inflicting repression; they may even mutiny. When all such events happen simultaneously, the persons who have been "rulers" become just other persons. This dissolution of power can happen in a wide variety of social and political conflicts.*
>
> *When people refuse cooperation, withhold their help, and persist in their disobedience and defiance, they are denying their opponents the basic human assistance and cooperation which any government or hierarchical system requires. If people do this in sufficient numbers for long enough, that government or hierarchical system will no longer have power. This is the basic political assumption of nonviolent action.*[2]

Exposure to Sharp's work was a pivotal intellectual moment for me, and in my continual commitment to the study of nonviolent action over the next four and half decades, I have never found an occasion to dispute its accuracy or revolutionary significance.

During the same period, I have come to appreciate the importance of accurate terminology to communicate about this phenomenon. Sharp used the term "nonviolent action," but I use the term "civil resistance." We mean the same thing, but part of why I prefer the term "civil resistance" is that it reduces the risk that people will conflate it with the concept of "nonviolence." "Nonviolence" refers to a moral position, while "civil resistance" refers to a strategy of conflict that uses nonviolent methods.

> ***"Nonviolence" refers to a moral position, while "civil resistance" refers to a strategy that uses nonviolent action to win power.***

Another example of terminological confusion in this field is the use of the term "protest movements" as a synonym for civil resistance. This ignores the fact that civil resistance incorporates many tactics other than mass protests—including strikes and

---

2   Gene Sharp, *The Politics of Nonviolent Action, Part One: Power and Struggle* (Boston, MA: Porter Sargent Publishers, 1973), 63.

TABLE 1

TERMS OF NONVIOLENT ACTION: EXPLAINED

The most frequently used terms that are synonymous with nonviolent action are **civil resistance** and **nonviolent conflict**. Synonyms that are less frequently used are **people power**, **nonviolent struggle**, and **nonviolent resistance**.

The term **nonviolent conflict** highlights the counterintuitive idea that nonviolent strategies and tactics can be successfully employed in conflicts against adversaries with well-equipped police and military.

Starting over a decade ago, the term **civil resistance** has been used with increasing frequency as a synonym for nonviolent conflict.

Other terms assumed to be synonymous with civil resistance campaigns are in fact sources of confusion. These include:

Peaceful dissent, which suggests ideas of tranquility, whereas nonviolent tactics are designed to disrupt the status quo in order to delegitimize tyrants.

Protest movements, which evokes dramatic images of millions of people in the streets, and yet no civil resistance campaign succeeds only with protests. A diverse array of tactics representing a carefully designed strategy is required.

Strategic nonviolence, is an ethical, moral, or religious precept that rejects violence and may remind us of the great moral leaders like Mohandas Gandhi and Martin Luther King, Jr. Yet many leaders of civil resistance campaigns may have been willing to engage in violent tactics if they believed it would help their cause. Instead, recognizing their circumstance they chose to maintain nonviolent discipline as a key component of a winning strategy.

Social justice movements, which can employ many of the same tactics but are designed through advocacy to change public opinion on specific issues like climate change, criminal justice reform, anti-racism, or same-sex marriage. Victory does not necessarily lead to a permanent recalibration of power relations. By way of contrast, the purpose of all campaigns of civil resistance is to defeat specific adversaries by undermining their base of power, particularly with respect to controlling an entire population.

In this volume, the term **civil resistance movement** is used interchangeably with the term **civil resistance campaign** as both convey human activity for a common purpose expressed in multiple stages over a period of time. The term **dissident** is used to refer to citizens struggling against the baleful effects of authoritarian oppression. These effects include perversion of the rule of law, corruption, loss of human rights, and all other systemic injustices that threaten life and liberty. Such people are also referred to as **pro-democracy activists**, and these terms will be used interchangeably.

The term **tyranny** is used interchangeably with the terms **dictatorship**, **authoritarianism**, and **despotism**. The leaders of these political systems are referred to as **tyrants**, **dictators**, **authoritarians**, and **despots**. The common feature of these regimes is their control of the levers of power in society leading to the systematic abuse of the human rights of their citizens.

It's useful here to distinguish between **civil resistance campaigns**, **tactics**, and **strategy**. A **civil resistance campaign** describes the entire history of a nonviolent conflict from the perspective of a dissident. **Tactics** describe the actions taken by violent and nonviolent protagonists at a specific time and place. **Strategy** is the linkage of tactics for maximum cumulative impact on the adversary.

For more explanations of nonviolent action terms, see Hardy Merriman and Nicola Barrach-Yousefi's *Glossary of Civil Resistance*, available for download from ICNC's website.

boycotts—which have played a decisive role in the history of non-violent action (for a sample, see Table 1, Terms of Nonviolent Action: Explained).

Sharp introduced an innovation that would prove to be of enormous benefit to our understanding of civil resistance. The entirety of *The Methods of Nonviolent Action*—the second volume of his seminal work, *The Politics of Nonviolent Action*—is devoted to the presentation of 198 methods (or tactics).[3] Without this list (and others that preceded it) nonviolent action would have remained an abstraction offering no practical insights for pro-democracy activists during real-time conflicts.[4]

In today's world, eleven of Sharp's tactics that are likely to prove the most damaging to a tyrant's ability to keep control are:

- Group or mass petition
- Assemblies of protest or support
- Withdrawal from social institutions
- Consumers' boycott of certain goods and services
- Deliberate inefficiency and selective noncooperation by constituent governmental units
- Producers' boycott (the refusal by producers to sell or otherwise deliver their own products)
- Refusal to pay fees, dues, and assessments
- Detailed strike (worker by worker, or by areas; piecemeal stoppages)
- Economic shutdown (when workers strike and employers simultaneously halt economic activities)
- Stay-in strike (occupation of worksite)
- Overloading of administrative systems

Under Sharp's tutelage, I wrote my doctoral thesis titled *Strategic Aspects of Nonviolent Resistance Movements*, which I successfully defended in 1976.

---

3   Gene Sharp, *The Politics of Nonviolent Action, Part Two: The Methods of Nonviolent Action* (Boston, MA: Porter Sargent Publishers, 1973).

4   See Krishnalal Shridharani, *War Without Violence: A Study of Gandhi's Method and Its Accomplishments* (New York: Harcourt, Brace and Co., 1939); and Martin Oppenheimer and George Lakey, *A Manual for Direct Action: Strategy and Tactics for Civil Rights and all other Nonviolent Protest Movements* (Chicago, IL: Quadrangle Books, 1965).

My thesis was inspired by an essay written by Professor Schelling over sixty years ago in the book *Civilian Resistance as a National Defence: Non-violent Action Against Aggression*. Schelling observed:

> *The tyrant and his subjects are in somewhat symmetrical positions. They can deny him most of what he wants—they can, that is, if they have the disciplined organization to refuse collaboration. And he can deny them just about everything they want—he can deny it by using the force at his command....It is a bargaining situation in which either side, if adequately disciplined and organized, can deny most of what the others wants; and it remains to see who wins.*[5]

According to Schelling the tactics that civil resisters choose have costs and benefits, as do the tactics used by their authoritarian opponents. The winner is the protagonist who distributes these costs and benefits most efficiently for their side. Skillful civil resisters want to create disruption in order to maximize defections from their opponent, and optimally want to employ tactics where relatively small disruptions lead to large numbers of defections. The skillful authoritarian needs to enforce obedience, often through violence, and optimally wants to use minimal violence to achieve maximum obedience. The cumulative aggregation of defection vis-à-vis obedience determines who wins.

I wanted to understand more fully who wins civil resistance campaigns and why.

Capitalizing on Schelling's insight, I hoped to expand the field of research about civil resistance from a study of power (i.e., a determination of which side has the most) to the study of strategy (i.e., a determination of which side is gaining the most). I wanted to understand more fully who wins campaigns of civil resistance and why. The purpose was never to create a predictive model but to highlight those features that may favor either side. My thesis compared two cases of nonviolent action that could not be more different: the First Russian Revolution from 1905 to 1907 and the Indian Independence Movement, with particular emphasis on the period of time from 1929 to 1931.

---

5   Thomas C. Schelling, "Some Questions on Civilian Defence," in *Civilian Resistance as a National Defence: Non-violent Action Against Aggression*, ed. Adam Roberts (Harrisburg, PA: Stackpole Books, 1968), 304.

The First Russian Revolution was a spontaneous mass nonviolent uprising with no leadership, but it achieved one early success against the tsar in the creation of the First Duma (parliament). Unfortunately, the movement was coopted by Bolsheviks and Mensheviks. It then degraded into sporadic acts of violence in Moscow and St. Petersburg that were easily suppressed by the tsar's forces, and the Duma was dissolved.

The Indian Independence Movement was led by Mohandas Gandhi, a charismatic figure uniquely capable of uniting Hindu and Muslim efforts to force the British out of India. Under his creative leadership, the 1930 Salt March mobilized over 250 million Indians. Related disruptions like the nonviolent raid on the Dharasana Salt Mines forced the viceroy into direct negotiations with Gandhi.

The vast difference in these two outcomes depended on three distinct decisions taken by each group of dissidents: whether to unify, whether to plan and execute a variety of tactics, and whether to maintain nonviolent discipline.

In the Russian Revolution the answer was "no" to all three decisions, while for the Indian Independence Movement the answer was "yes" to all three decisions. These were decisions taken freely by the dissidents and not by their authoritarian adversaries. Also, it was impossible to argue which authoritarian—the Russian tsar or the Indian viceroy—was more skillful in protecting their status because both were extremely disoriented by events. Therefore, it is fair to conclude the following: First, the skills of the Indians in waging nonviolent conflict were superior to those of the Russians, and second, that Professor Schelling is correct that the dissident who is the most "adequately disciplined and organized" vis-à-vis his authoritarian adversary has the best possible chances of winning.

In battles between dissidents and tyrants, skills are the prime determinant of who wins a nonviolent conflict.

This offers insight into an ongoing social science debate over what causes events to occur: structure (i.e., conditions) or agency (i.e., skills).

I believe a compelling case has been made that in battles between dissidents and tyrants, skills are the prime determinant of who wins a nonviolent conflict. The overwhelming majority of so-called political realists find this conclusion ridiculous given the monopoly of weapons available to every tyrant. Yet think of its implication: If prior conditional advantages are poor predictors of success or failure for dissidents, then their skills in waging civil resistance campaigns become critically important. They can actually redraw the limitations seemingly imposed on them from the period before a nonviolent conflict begins until the moment it ends. This is why communicating this hopeful news to pro-democracy activists and other relevant constituencies has been a major commitment of my career.

The evidence supporting this view is abundant. From the time of Mohandas Gandhi to the US Civil Rights Movement, from Cold War–era struggles for democracy in Eastern Europe to the anti-apartheid struggle in South Africa, the history of nations has been shaped by civil resistance campaigns. Recent decades have witnessed the acceleration of a new generation of movements and leadership in places like Algeria, Armenia, Bahrain, Burkina Faso, Egypt, Georgia, Guatemala, Hong Kong, Iran, Lebanon, Myanmar, Nepal, Nicaragua, Pakistan, Poland, Russia, Serbia, Slovakia, Sudan, Togo, Tunisia, Ukraine, Venezuela, and Zimbabwe.

Popular nonviolent mobilization in many of these countries has eroded the strength of tyrants, reversed democratic backsliding, curtailed corruption, bolstered societal resilience, and advanced human rights for women, minorities, and other threatened groups. While not all movements succeed or consolidate gains (for example, in Bahrain or Egypt), and some remain ongoing (for example, in Iran, Myanmar, Venezuela, and Zimbabwe), a strong body of historic evidence shows that civil resistance movements are the single largest driver of democratic transitions from authoritarian rule. Tyrants do not say so publicly, but this is the scenario that they fear most. Their Achilles heel is strategically sound, popular, and sustained civil resistance by the populations they attempt to rule and repress.

Gene Sharp believed—and I still do—that civil resistance had been and would continue to be relevant to conflicts against tyrants in every corner of the world. In 1983, we founded the Albert Einstein Institution (AEI) to disseminate knowledge about this field with dissidents who were at risk of repression while in the heat of battle.

Recognizing that our best option was to promote general knowledge and insights about how to effectively wage campaigns of civil resistance, we did not offer specific tactical advice. Telling dissidents

From left-to-right: Peter Ackerman, Gene Sharp, and Lithuanian Minister of Defense Audrius Butkevičius in Vilnius, 1991.

to "first strike here, then protest there" was too dangerous. The strategy and tactics of each nonviolent conflict is uniquely shaped by its country's culture, religion, economics, and other factors that can only be appreciated by indigenous leadership. Before offering advice, we acknowledged our own ignorance of their battlefield, including the intentions and capabilities of the violent adversaries they faced.

Nevertheless, on rare occasions we did enter conflict zones to be of assistance to nonviolent protagonists. One memorable experience was our visit in 1991 to Lithuania to meet with the prime minister and minister of defense. Russian troops had recently entered the country, and in one confrontation at the main TV station in Vilnius there were over 150 Lithuanian casualties. The opposition wanted an alternative strategy to armed defense in order to counter the full-scale invasion that they feared was imminent.

Today the Lithuanian government has in place a well-developed plan for mass civil resistance against possible foreign occupation.

During this encounter and many others that followed, I met dissidents that believed they were facing tremendous odds against their tyrannical adversaries. Nevertheless, they eagerly sought advice as to how they could discover for themselves their optimal nonviolent strategy.

Expanding beyond the work of the Albert Einstein Institution, I also supported the development of several films about civil resistance. One of these was the Emmy-nominated documentary *A Force More Powerful*, for which I was the principal content advisor. It was broadcast nationally on US public television (PBS) in September 2000, and told six stories of nonviolent resistance:

- The Indian Independence Movement against British rule in the 1930s

- The US Civil Rights movement in the 1960s

- The South African anti-apartheid struggle in the mid-1980s

- The Danish Resistance to Nazi occupation in the early-1940s

- The Chilean workers opposition to the rule of General Augusto Pinochet in the 1980s

- The Polish Solidarity Movement for independent unions and democratic rights in 1980

The message underlying *A Force More Powerful* is that despite these conflicts, occurring on different continents and during different decades, they all tell the same story. They reveal how nonviolent tactics can be sequenced into a coherent strategy to disintegrate the power of even the most repressive authoritarian adversary.

The second film I co-produced, *Bringing Down a Dictator,* aired on PBS in 2002. It told the story of how Slobodan Milosevic, the "Butcher of the Balkans," was forced from office by popular, organized civil resistance. Contrary to popular opinion, his total loss of power occurred without a single shot being fired.

Bringing Down a Dictator won a Peabody Award for documentary excellence in 2002 and in the same year was selected by the International Documentary Association as the best documentary of that year. In combination with two other award-winning documentaries on civil resistance these films have been translated in over 20 languages and dialects.[6] They have been viewed by millions of people in over 100 countries.

---

6   *Orange Revolution* documents events Ukraine in 2004 and *Egypt: Revolution Interrupted?* documents events in Egypt in the years before and after the Egyptian revolution in 2011. All films can be streamed for free from https://www.nonviolent-conflict.org/icncfilms/.

The success of these movies confirmed there was a far greater demand for civil resistance knowledge than the Albert Einstein Institution (AEI) was prepared to address. Sharp wanted AEI to focus primarily on his work, and I wanted to be more aggressive in creating and distributing knowledge to pro-democracy activists. In 2002, I founded the International Center on Nonviolent Conflict (ICNC) to support original research and share knowledge in this field in order to advance democratic governance consistent with the Universal Declaration of Human Rights.

ICNC's theory of change is based on this three-part model:

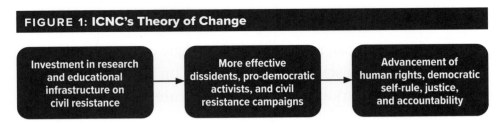

FIGURE 1: ICNC's Theory of Change

Investment in research and educational infrastructure on civil resistance → More effective dissidents, pro-democratic activists, and civil resistance campaigns → Advancement of human rights, democratic self-rule, justice, and accountability

This model emphasizes that the existence of more knowledgeable dissidents and pro-democracy activists is vital to humanity's progress. It also recognizes that tyranny must be faced and challenged if it is to be transformed. Tyranny produces the most inhumane conditions imaginable leading to widespread violence, death, disasters, uncontrolled disease, poverty, ignorance, and corruption. Addressing these issues can only occur by recalibrating the power relationship between dictators and their citizens.

Civil resistance enables populations to fight against tyranny in a way that maximizes their probability of success while minimizing potential loss of life. Data-driven research shows that civil resistance has the greatest potential to lead to stable democratic transitions that result in political, social, and economic development.

Furthermore, campaigns of civil resistance are far more frequent than generally realized, with over 150 new campaigns emerging thus far in the current century, including 95 new campaigns that began between 2010 and 2019. In this same period, the number of new civil resistance campaigns far exceeds the number of new violent insurgencies (see Figure 2).

However, there is a paradox: Even though civil resistance has become the preferred strategy of liberation around the world, its success rates have dramatically declined (see Figure 3).

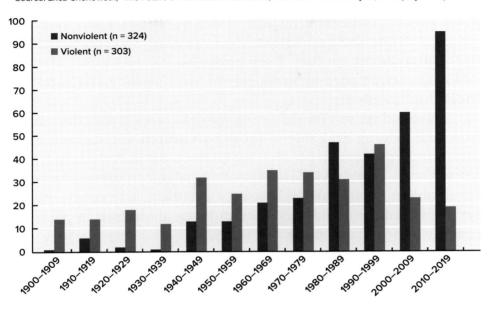

FIGURE 2: Onsets of Nonviolent and Violent Mass Campaigns by Decade (1900–2019)

Source: Erica Chenoweth, "The Future of Nonviolent Resistance," *Journal of Democracy* 31, no. 3 (July 2020): 69–84.

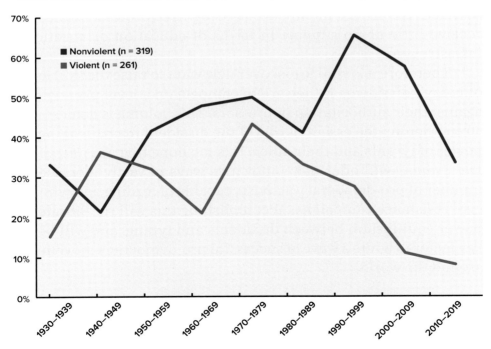

FIGURE 3: Success Rates of Nonviolent and Violent Mass Campaigns by Decade (1930–2019)

Source: Erica Chenoweth, "The Future of Nonviolent Resistance," *Journal of Democracy* 31, no. 3 (July 2020): 69–84.

One reason for this decline is that dictators have increased their skills at confronting and countering challenges to their power by pro-democracy activists. For example, tyrants have become more adept at undermining unity among dissidents and inducing violence within their ranks, thereby reducing public participation in the nonviolent conflict. They have also become more adept at utilizing cutting edge technologies to limit privacy and suppress individual freedoms.

A second reason for declining success rates is that the education and training available to those committed to civil resistance has not kept pace with the frequency of these campaigns. Information about civil resistance campaigns continues to prove invaluable for dissidents, whose greatest obstacle in confronting a tyrant is confusion and lack of confidence about how to plan and execute a winning strategy.

Unfortunately, the number of dissidents with access to usable knowledge about civil resistance is currently a tiny fraction of the existing demand.

Career professionals like medical doctors or soldiers undergo extensive education and training to hone their skills and expertise. This enables them to perform and succeed despite highly stressful and adversarial conditions. In contrast, dissidents and pro-democracy activists are not members of a recognized profession and thus receive little or no support in terms of education or vocational infrastructure.

Therefore it is vital to discover new ways to raise the skill levels of today's dissidents if they are to compete on a level playing field against their authoritarian oppressors. This volume is dedicated to strengthening the essential role of the dissident in challenging the power of tyrants and their allies. It is my hope that *The Checklist to End Tyranny* will offer new innovative ways to vastly increase the number of pro-democracy activists capable of leading and winning civil resistance campaigns. Accomplishing this will recalibrate the power equilibrium between dissidents and tyrants and will be the key factor to ignite a wave of successful pro-democracy movements around the world.

At right: Orange Revolution demonstrators in Kyiv, Ukraine, 2004.

Nonviolent conflicts are best understood as competitions for power between dissidents and tyrants. When a civil resistance campaign is finished, there will be one winner and one loser determined by which side has superior skills.

Chapter Two

OVERCOMING FEAR AND CONFUSION:

Five Ideas Dissidents Must Know

Over the last eighteen years, the International Center on Nonviolent Conflict (ICNC) has accelerated the dissemination of knowledge about civil resistance to the global public. Through films, workshops, lectures, and the promotion of research, we have interacted with dissidents, scholars, media professionals, foreign policy professionals, public officials, and members of the international NGO community. Our website (www.nonviolent-conflict.org) is a global clearinghouse of information on civil resistance, with resources translated in over 70 different languages and dialects—a list that is continuously expanding (see Table 2).

Most importantly, we have had significant engagement with thousands of dissidents and pro-democracy activists from more than 100 countries on every continent (see Figure 4).

Our intended impact is to show how widespread distribution of knowledge about civil resistance reduces levels of deadly violence in conflict and improves prospects for democratic rule free from corruption and in support of basic human rights.

These activities were recognized when ICNC was nominated in 2014 for the Nobel Peace Prize. Among the signers were: Lech Walesa, the head of the Solidarity Movement in Poland and himself a Nobel Peace Prize Winner; Thomas Schelling, the 2005 Nobel Laureate in Economics; Larry Diamond, a preeminent scholar on the state of democracy in the world; James Stavridis, the first naval officer to be the NATO Supreme Allied Commander in Europe; and Rev. James

TABLE 2: The 74 Languages in ICNC's Resource Library					
Afaan Oromo	Crimean Tatar	Hebrew	Kurdish	Norwegian	Tagalog
Amharic		Hindi	Kyrgyz	Pashto	Tamil
Arabic	Croatian	Hungarian	Latvian	Polish	Telugu
Armenian	Dari	Indonesian	Lingala	Portuguese (Brazilian)	Thai
Azeri	Dutch	Italian	Lithuanian		Tibetan
Balochi	English	Japanese	Luganda	Portuguese (Continental)	Tigrinya
Bangla	Estonian	Jing-Paw	Macedonian	Russian	Turkish
Belarusian	Farsi	Kannada	Malagasy	Serbian	Ukrainian
Bosnian	French	Karen	Malayalam	Sindhi	Urdu
Burmese	Georgian	Khmer	Mayan	Slovak	Uzbek
Catalan	German	Kirundi	Mon	Spanish	Vietnamese
Chin	Gujarati	Kituba	Mongolian	Swahili	Xhosa
Chinese	Haitian Creole	Korean	Nepali		

Lawson, a leading strategist of the US Civil Rights Movement and organizer of the Nashville lunch counter sit-ins in 1960 (see Table 3).

It has been our experience that whatever their origin, dissidents living under tyranny share common challenges. As pro-democracy activists they are restricted to three choices, two of which are either unpalatable or filled with unknown risks. The typical dissident has already rejected the option of passivity or acquiescence with the status quo of lost freedom. With a few exceptions they also have little confidence in mounting a violent insurrection. Some have already been involved with a failing violent insurrection and want to consider alternative strategies.

This leaves the third option of civil resistance, about which dissidents harbor two almost contradictory beliefs. First, they believe a campaign of nonviolent resistance may be their last best hope for winning their freedom and rights. Second, they wonder whether their unique circumstance makes a campaign of civil resistance futile. Above all, pro-democracy activists are desperate to find ideas they can believe in. As with all forms of competition, confidence is critical to thinking clearly, acting decisively, and remaining resilient. Whoever—whether dissident or tyrant—has the most confidence in their strategy, assuming their strategy is viable, is likely to prevail in nonviolent conflict.

This is why it is critical that at first contact, five distinct ideas are conveyed to dissidents to reduce fear and create positive expectations for winning against their tyrannical adversaries.

We the undersigned ... nominating for the 2014 Peace Prize *the premier organization sharing knowledge of how to pursue* justice without violence — *a group comprised of scholar-activists that has for the past eleven years strengthened, deepened, and widened the dissemination of* reliable, practical information *based on tangible results, meticulous scholarship, and dependable historical data. Put more simply, we are nominating the group that has been making the understanding of* nonviolent action *graspable throughout the world.... Ideas do not teach themselves, and people learn ideas and their practical lessons most efficiently when they have access to experienced practitioners, thinkers, and the* best materials available.

ICNC has led the way *in the 21st century in the systematic study and global teaching of the dynamics,* effective strategies *and best practices of civil resistance movements. We believe that the velocity with which* knowledge of civil resistance *has encircled the world over the last decade is largely attributable to their original work. Without their efforts, this vital global front in the* expansion of peace, *not only among nations but within them, would not have come into existence in such an organized and sustained way.*

Signed by Lech Walesa, Thomas Schelling, Larry Diamond, James Stavridis, James Lawson, among others

This map indicates countries and territories (in yellow) from which ICNC has had at least one participant attend an in-person workshop or seminar of at least four days in length. In a significant majority of these countries ICNC has had multiple engagements with participants over a period of many years.

Afghanistan	Bolivia	Cameroon	Democratic Republic of Congo	Ethiopia	Guinea (Conakry)	Indonesia
Algeria	Bosnia and Herzegovina	Canada		Fiji	Greece	Iran
Argentina		Chile	Dominican Republic	Finland	Guatemala	Iraq
Armenia	Brazil	China		France	Haiti	Israel
Australia	Bulgaria	Colombia	Ecuador	Gambia	Honduras	Italy
Austria	Burkina Faso	Cote d'Ivoire (Ivory Coast)	Egypt	Georgia	Hong Kong	Jordan
Bangladesh	Burma		El Salvador	Germany	Hungary	Kazakhstan
Belarus	Burundi		Estonia	Ghana	India	Kenya
Belgium	Cambodia					Kosovo

Kuwait	Mauritania	Nicaragua	Russia	South Sudan	Tibet	Uruguay
Kyrgyzstan	Mexico	Nigeria	Senegal	Spain	Tonga	Vanuatu
Lebanon	Moldova	Norway	Serbia	Sri Lanka	Tunisia	Venezuela
Liberia	Mongolia	Pakistan	Sierra Leone	Sudan	Turkey	Vietnam
Libya	Morocco	Palestine	Singapore	Sweden	Uganda	West Papua
Macedonia	Namibia	Paraguay	Slovakia	Switzerland	Ukraine	Western Sahara
Madagascar	Nepal	Peru	Slovenia	Syria	United	Yemen
Malawi	Netherlands	Philippines	Somalia	Tanzania	Kingdom	Zambia
Maldives	New Zealand	Poland	South Africa	Thailand	United States	Zimbabwe

TABLE 4

5 IDEAS DISSIDENTS MUST KNOW:

1 Dissidents should take solace in the historical fact that they are traveling a road many have traveled before and many others will travel in the future.

2 Dissidents must realize that there is nothing about the circumstances of their specific conflict that precludes their success.

3 Strategies based on violent tactics have a low probability of winning because they have limited pathways to victory. By way of contrast, rejecting violent tactics and maintaining nonviolent discipline creates more possible pathways to victory.

4 A campaign of civil resistance is the most reliable driver of democratic transitions.

5 The most important thing dissidents can do to improve their chances of success is to develop their skills of organizing, mobilizing, and resisting, so they are superior to those of their authoritarian adversary.

IDEA #1

Dissidents should take solace in the historical fact that they are traveling a road many have traveled before and many others will travel in the future.

In the past, case studies about civil resistance were not always readily available. For example, in 1976 my dissertation was a comparative study of two cases. Sixteen years later, my first book, *Strategic Nonviolent Conflict: The Dynamics of People Power in the Twentieth Century*, compared six cases. In 2000, my second book, *A Force More Powerful: A Century of Nonviolent Conflict*, studied only thirteen cases.

In 2007, ICNC began funding the development of the Nonviolent and Violent Campaigns and Outcomes (NAVCO) Data Project, which led to the award-winning 2011 book *Why Civil Resistance Works: The Strategic Logic of Nonviolent Conflict* by Erica Chenoweth and Maria Stephan.[7] The book analyzed 106 cases of nonviolent campaigns between 1900 and 2006 and gave quantitative affirmation to the superior effectiveness of civil resistance versus violent insurgency in challenging brutal regimes.

Since 2011, the NAVCO Data Project has continued to add cases of nonviolent conflict totaling 325 as of the end of 2019. The database is open source, and pro-democracy activists can easily find similar cases that resonate with their own.[8] This project has also expanded to include daily observations from within campaigns, so that we can better understand the way short-term interactions can impact the direction that campaigns take. Cumulatively, total data entries are in the millions.

The publication of the book *Why Civil Resistance Works* created enormous worldwide credibility and interest in nonviolent conflict as a field of study. Furthermore, the data upon which it is based provides confirmation of the wisdom, but not the uniqueness, of the decision to begin a campaign of civil resistance.

---

7   *Why Civil Resistance Works: The Strategic Logic of Nonviolent Conflict* won the 2012 Woodrow Wilson Foundation Award from the American Political Science Association for the best book on government, politics, or international affairs.

8   NAVCO data project is currently hosted by Harvard University at: https://dataverse.harvard.edu/dataverse/navco

IDEA #2

Dissidents must realize that there is nothing about the circumstances of their specific conflict that precludes their success.

Afrequent refrain, particularly from foreign policy professionals, is that nonviolent resistance only succeeds against benign or mildly contentious adversaries and will fail to succeed in societies that are either poor or rife with ethnic divisions. Consistently overlooked is the defeat of the apartheid regime in South Africa, the Pinochet dictatorship in Chile, the Marcos dictatorship in the Philippines, and the communist regime in Poland. More recent examples include the fall of Hosni Mubarak in Egypt, Zine El Abidine Ben Ali in Tunisia, and Omar al-Bashir in Sudan, who is one of the twenty-first century's most brutal dictators. None of these tyrannical regimes can be claimed to have been mild, benign, or unwilling to use severe repression, even mass killings. None of these countries featured growing economies. These cases also include societies with high degrees of ethnic and cultural diversity.

Some skeptics respond saying, "Surely you don't think that totalitarian governments like the North Korean or Chinese regimes can fall as easily?" First, there is nothing easy about the fall of any tyranny. Second, it is important to remember that tyrannies are not always as strong as they appear, and their power can erode even when they appear to outsiders to be in control. As one saying goes, when tyrannies last, they look invincible; when they fall, their downfall is suddenly seen as inevitable. Third, the longevity of an autocratic regime depends on the tyrant's ability to have a strategy to stay in power. Regarding North Korea and China, societies in both of these countries are hardly static or withdrawn—otherwise why would these regimes need so many oppressive measures to keep people obedient? In such dynamic societies, early phases of civil resistance can begin to loosen the grip of a tyrant on the population. Successive waves of nonviolent conflict can then increase the probability of winning.

These qualitative examples are supported by quantitative analysis. In 2008, the organization Freedom House issued a research study, *Enabling Environments for Civic Movements and the Dynamics of Democratic Transition*, that examined various structural factors and their influence on civil resistance in 67 transitions from authoritarian to democratic rule between 1975 and 2006.

[N]either the political nor environmental factors examined in the study had a statistically significant impact on the success or failure of civil resistance movements.... [C]ivic movements are as likely to succeed in less developed, economically poor countries as in developed, affluent societies. The study also finds no significant evidence that ethnic or religious polarization has a major impact on the possibilities for the emergence of a cohesive civic opposition. Nor does regime type seem to have an important influence on the ability of civic movements to achieve broad support.[9]

IDEA #3

Strategies based on violent tactics have a low probability of winning because they have limited pathways to victory. By way of contrast, rejecting violent tactics and maintaining nonviolent discipline creates more possible pathways to victory.

There are two reasons for this conclusion. One is structural and one is based on quantitative research. Regarding the structural reason, please see Figure 5, in which the population is divided into four parts. The first is the most senior stratum of leadership who are the greatest beneficiaries of the regime's tyranny. The second are the

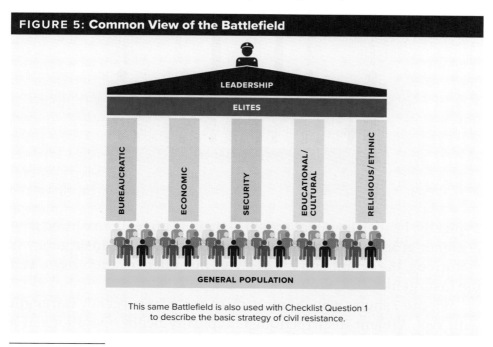

FIGURE 5: **Common View of the Battlefield**

This same Battlefield is also used with Checklist Question 1 to describe the basic strategy of civil resistance.

---

9 Eleanor Marchant and Arch Puddington, *Enabling Environments for Civic Movements and the Dynamics of Democratic Transition* (Washington, DC: Freedom House, July 2008), 1.

elites from every part of society that give the leadership leverage to execute their oppressive mandates. The third are the workers and managers from each pillar of support required for a functioning society. Pillars vary by country and culture, and the only constant is the pillar representing the security forces. The fourth is the general population. Some citizens within the general population are responsible for maintaining and serving the pillars. Others are working in the less formal areas of society that are harder to identify and control.

In the theory of violent insurrection (as seen in Figure 6), guerrilla forces are activated to kill key members of society who maintain the pillars of support. They then move up to kill members of the elite until the security forces can no longer protect the leadership.

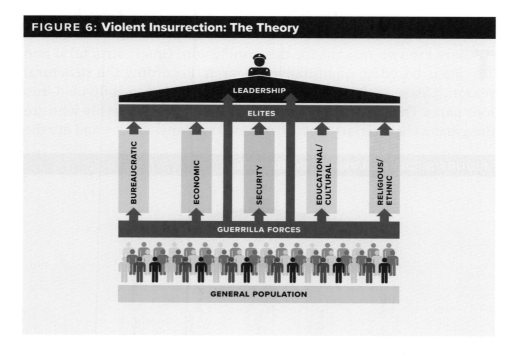

FIGURE 6: **Violent Insurrection: The Theory**

Typically, in such a violent scenario there is no real remaining government group to negotiate a power transfer. If the insurgency is victorious, the tyrant and his acolytes must flee for their lives, and the insurgents take power.

Figure 7 shows why the strategy of armed insurgency is fraught with risk. Violent insurrectionists typically begin operations at a steep military disadvantage to the tyrant's security forces. Unless the violent insurrectionists have early and significant victories, their military capabilities will quickly deteriorate. Given enough time, the tyrant's security forces will circle the wagons to protect their key supporters and counterattack to wipe out the violent insurrectionists.

Of course, the negative impacts will be felt most by the general population, which experiences significant collateral damage from armed struggle. Furthermore, a failed violent insurrection can render the population quiescent for years, making them reluctant to undertake any measure of resistance, including any reliance on nonviolent tactics to oppose the tyrant.

The relative futility of violent insurrection is corroborated by data from many cases. Several points are worth our consideration:

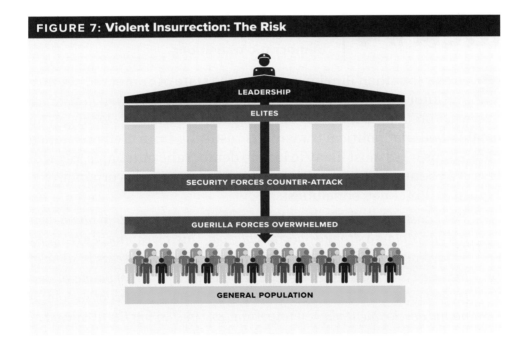

FIGURE 7: Violent Insurrection: The Risk

LEADERSHIP

ELITES

SECURITY FORCES COUNTER-ATTACK

GUERILLA FORCES OVERWHELMED

GENERAL POPULATION

- Over the last 120 years, nonviolent conflicts have had a success rate at least twice that of violent insurrections.
- The average duration of a successful nonviolent insurrection is three years, versus nine years for a successful violent insurrection.
- Mass killings of a thousand civil resisters or more are approximately three times more likely to occur during a violent insurrection than during a civil resistance campaign.

- A winning campaign of civil resistance can be as much as nine times more likely to transition to a democratic outcome than with a tyranny overthrown by a violent insurrection.

- Even when a civil resistance campaign fails, there is still a 35 percent chance that it will succeed in transitioning to a democratic outcome within the next five years. This resilience stands in stark contrast to a failed violent insurrection, which has virtually no chance of succeeding five years later.[10]

This data makes clear that it is irrational to inject violence into an insurrection against a tyrant and that a civil resistance campaign has a far better risk vs. return.

IDEA #4 | A campaign of civil resistance is the most reliable driver of democratic transitions.

Scholar Jonathan Pinckney studies the state of democracy before and after nonviolent conflicts. In his study, *When Civil Resistance Succeeds: Building Democracy After Popular Nonviolent Uprisings,* he established that political transitions resulting from civil resistance campaigns were most likely to lead to democratic outcomes, regardless of a country's pre-transition state of democratic governance (see Figure 8). Pinckney concludes:

> *The statistical evidence strongly supports the contention that nonviolent resistance plays a strong democratizing role. This role cannot be explained by favorable conditions. Civil resistance occurs and succeeds in some of the worst and most repressive regimes. It is not a foolproof panacea, and factors like a country's regional political context or level of socio-economic development play an important role in shaping the likelihood of democratization. However, even in extremely undemocratic countries, civil resistance dramatically shapes a country's political transition, leading to a much higher likelihood of democratization.*[11]

This finding is vital information for dissidents. It is also relevant for the world's assumption about how democracy is advanced and protected.

---

10   Consult Peter Ackerman and Hardy Merriman's *Preventing Mass Atrocities: From a Responsibility to Protect (RtoP) to a Right to Assist (RtoA) Campaigns of Civil Resistance* for a discussion of these data points, available as a free download from www.nonviolent-conflict.org.

11   Jonathan Pinckney, *When Civil Resistance Succeeds: Building Democracy After Popular Nonviolent Uprisings* (Washington, DC: ICNC Press, 2018), 40.

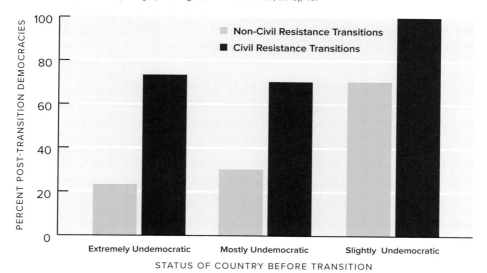

FIGURE 8: Pre-Transition Levels of Democracy and Post-Transition Democracy

Source: Jonathan Pinckney, *When Civil Resistance Succeeds: Building Democracy After Popular Nonviolent Uprisings* (Washington, DC: ICNC Press, 2018), 40.

IDEA #5

The most important thing dissidents can do to improve their chances of success is to develop their skills of organizing, mobilizing, and resisting, so they are superior to those of their authoritarian adversary.

Campaigns of civil resistance are best understood as competitions for power between dissidents (and the populations they represent) and tyrants. When the nonviolent conflict is over, there will be one winner and one loser determined by which side had superior skills.

By way of analogy, think of any athletic event, whether it be tennis, wrestling, basketball, or football. If the desire to win on both sides is intensely felt, then the two individuals or teams will try to outmatch each other in their preparations for the competition. In every significant sport, billions of dollars have been spent on facilities to accommodate athletes and their coaches.

Consider the exemplary career of a military figure such as retired four-star admiral James Stavridis. As a former Supreme Allied Commander at NATO, he commanded a navy destroyer, a destroyer squadron, and an aircraft carrier battle group in combat. When I asked the Admiral how many hours of training he had versus his hours in command, his reply was "6 to 1." Also, the education and training hours are almost entirely skewed to the early and middle parts of his career. Admiral Stavridis is a graduate of the United States Naval Academy and other prestigious war colleges. As part of his training, he received a PhD in international affairs from the Fletcher School of Law and Diplomacy.

Does anyone think dissidents have anywhere near the equivalent ratio of training to operations in their own careers? Are there any venerable institutions specifically tasked with enhancing a dissident's capabilities along a predictable career path? Most citizens assume the role of dissident after having just left or while holding an unrelated occupation. Where is the leadership expertise gained prior to undertaking civil resistance against a tyrant? The tyrant's greatest asset is not his military strength; it is his ability to sow fear and confusion among pro-democracy activists. The result can be passivity when a campaign of civil resistance is desperately needed.

By accepting the five ideas in this chapter, dissidents can lay the foundation for their own in-depth learning about civil resistance.

ICNC has been the leader in creating opportunities for educating dissidents and pro-democracy activists to develop their understanding of civil resistance. Five-day workshops and seven-week online courses have been ICNC's key educational formats for the advanced interdisciplinary study of civil resistance. Since 2006 we have had participants in these events from over 130 countries and territories (see Figure 9, opposite).

During these sessions, activists, scholars, journalists, and members of nongovernmental organizations and policy communities from every continent except Antarctica have closely collaborated. They all share the pursuit of a deeper understanding of how civil resistance movements form, organize, strategize, mobilize, build coalitions, communicate, select tactics, negotiate, and create change. Taught by leading international scholars and veterans of past civil resistance campaigns, these programs cover a wide variety of issues, including the role of external actors in supporting or suppressing civil resistance, the challenges of democratic transitions, and strategies that movements use to respond to violent repression and armed insurgency.

Much is at stake when it comes to the quality of these workshops. After years of interaction with so many dissidents, we have

Afghanistan American Samoa Argentina Armenia
Australia BANGLADESH Belarus Belgium Benin
Bosnia Azerbaijan Burkina Faso Burma Bolivia
Cambodia Brazil Bulgaria Burundi
Cameroon CANADA Chile China Colombia
Cuba Czech Republic Democratic Republic of Congo
DENMARK Djibouti East Timor East Turkestan ECUADOR
Egypt El Salvador Eritrea Estonia Ethiopia Fiji
Finland France Gambia Germany Ghana Greece
GEORGIA
Guatemala Guinea Haiti Honduras Hong Kong
Hungary India Indonesia Iran Ireland ISRAEL
Italy Japan Jordan Kashmir Iraq Kazakhstan

ICNC ONLINE COURSE PARTICIPANTS BY PLACE OF ORIGIN

Kenya Kosovo Kuwait Kyrgyzstan Laos Lebanon Liberia
MACEDONIA Madagascar MALAYSIA Maldives
Marshall Islands Mauritania Mexico Moldova Morocco Nepal
Netherlands New Zealand Nigeria NORWAY Pakistan
Palestine Papua New Guinea Paraguay Peru
Philippines Poland PORTUGAL Qatar Romania
Russia Rwanda SAUDI ARABIA Serbia Sierra Leone
Singapore Slovakia Solomon Islands South Africa
South Sudan Spain Sri Lanka Sudan South Korea
& Catalonia SWEDEN
Switzerland Syria Taiwan Tanzania Thailand Tibet Togo
Tonga TUNISIA Turkey Uganda Ukraine United Kingdom
United States Uzbekistan Vanuatu VENEZUELA Vietnam
WEST PAPUA Western Sahara Yemen Zambia Zimbabwe

FIGURE 9: ICNC ONLINE COURSE PARTICIPANTS BY PLACE OF ORIGIN   **33**

consistently observed that the biggest asset available to a tyrant is not his military resources. Instead it is the number of social, economic, and political variables that pro-democracy activists have to contend with that can easily result in their confusion, apathy, and division, to the resounding benefit of the tyrant. The environments in which nonviolent conflicts are fought are complex, and civil resisters—requiring grassroots and coalition-based coordination to sequence an array of tactics into a strategy for winning—often experience a sense of disorientation. Their natural fear of making the wrong decisions with people's lives and freedoms on the line can induce the very passivity that a tyrant seeks, and also bolster the illusion of a tyrant's invincibility.

This is why feedback has been vital to help ICNC understand how alumni have responded to the knowledge and support they have received. To this end, ICNC has collected hundreds of written and verbal evaluations by program participants, grantees, and collaborators that assess impact. Here are some of the key findings:

TABLE 5: Key Findings from Participant Evaluations

- **ICNC's educational programs and content are unique in the NGO sector, highly useful, and unlike any other training or workshop that most participants have ever attended.**

- **As a result of ICNC's programs and grants, participants report that they are:**
  - a. **more engaged in and effective at civil resistance and movement organizing;**
  - b. **applying what they learned in their fields of practice; and**
  - c. **teaching this knowledge to others.**

- **Long-term collaborations and solidarity networks have emerged between participants who met and learned together at ICNC events.**

- **In some cases, civil resistance campaigns for human rights have emerged out of ICNC programs and grant support.**

Please see the Appendix which provides additional evaluation data and a typical five-day agenda.

Positive recognition has also come from key experts, including U.S. Civil Rights Movement leader Dr. James Lawson, who organized the 1960s Nashville lunch counter sit-ins. Dr. Lawson has trained thousands of people over the last six decades, has taught at several universities, and recently won the Congressional Gold Medal:

> *This is an agency that I guess I have often wished for to happen. It has done more to disseminate and propagate and spread the word about the emergence of nonviolent struggle, nonviolent actions, civil resistance, and the like than any in the last 100 years.... [I]t has done more for the work of getting people to recognize their own options to the present world, that there are options for how we fight and how we resist wrong and to show forth the fact that these options are not written in empty dreams but written in the concrete work of millions, if not billions, of people across the last 120 years....*

Reverend Lawson attended a 2016 workshop and said ICNC's work was "the most critical work in my own country and in Western civilization, period."

Undoubtedly one of the reasons these workshops have been so successful is the intimacy of the setting (or, for online courses, the depth of engagement) and the thoroughness of the curriculum. Students receive tremendous reinforcement by being with others from many different countries in the region dealing with the same hopes and fears.

But what happens after a workshop or online course is over and the dissidents return to the heat of battle in their home country? They may be highly satisfied with their experience, but they did not come to the workshops to receive knowledge for themselves alone. Depending on their activities, hundreds if not thousands of their fellow citizens may rely on the information gained from the workshop. Therefore insights must be clear and straightforward and able to be transmitted accurately and with ease in order to be used effectively by those not in attendance.

The importance of this, and other questions related to knowledge sharing and application, should not be underestimated. We are now at a pivotal moment in history as authoritarianism rises globally and the number of nonviolent pro-democracy movements increases dramatically. The simultaneous existence of these two trends explains the explosion in demand by dissidents for educational assistance in making their movements more powerful.

This has created the need to transmit information without ICNC's direct involvement and to make the information usable on a day-to-day basis. To do this, dissidents should be provided with additional tools to support them becoming their own educators and coaches. "The Checklist Exercise for Freedom" described in Chapter 5 can be a groundbreaking way to make this happen. The foundation for this exercise is a checklist of eight questions described in Chapters 3 and 4.

The Checklist Questions provide a clear basis for dissidents to evaluate their campaign's current state of competitiveness. They can help pinpoint strengths, weaknesses, and the key areas that need focus and adjustment. In an environment with multiple demands on pro-democracy activists, such analysis can significantly narrow the margins for failure. The Checklist can help dissidents cut through a sense of disorientation and navigate a path forward with an impressive measure of confidence.

> *The Checklist reveals how and why civil resistance campaigns fail or win and how to identify alternative tactical pathways.*

The eight questions in the Checklist fall into two categories: "Building Capabilities" and "Navigating Conflict." They are designed to yield a subjective response that is less about current status and more about momentum into the future. Answers to each checklist question will be "Yes" or "No," but with different and changing degrees of intensity as the nonviolent conflict unfolds.

Answers to the above questions should invite careful consideration by individual dissidents as well as organized groups of pro-democracy activists.

Some may claim that with so many variables in play, a checklist for ending tyranny is too reductionist. They may argue that critical decision making during future nonviolent conflicts requires primary attention to factors unique to a particular time and place.

The Checklist does not call for ignoring specific factors in a conflict. Instead the Checklist promotes understanding of those factors in the context of a broader strategic framework. The Checklist should reveal to dissidents how and why their civil resistance campaign can fail or win and how to identify alternative tactical pathways.

Developing a checklist aimed at helping civil resistance campaigns fight against tyranny is no small task. If poorly conceived, it can literally have life and death consequences.

However, in many other fields of endeavor where there are great complexities—like multi-use real estate developments or life and

TABLE 6

THE **CHECKLIST** TO END TYRANNY:

BUILDING CAPABILITIES

1 Is the civil resistance campaign unifying around aspirations, leaders, and a strategy for winning?

2 Is the civil resistance campaign diversifying its tactical options while maintaining nonviolent discipline?

3 Is the civil resistance campaign sequencing tactics for maximum disruption with minimum risk?

4 Is the civil resistance campaign discovering ways to make external support more valuable?

NAVIGATING CONFLICT

5 Are the number and diversity of citizens confronting the tyranny likely to grow?

6 Is the tyrant's belief in the efficacy of violent repression likely to diminish?

7 Are potential defectors among the tyrant's key supporters likely to increase?

8 Is a post-conflict political order likely to emerge consistent with democratic values?

death issues such as with aviation and emergency medicine—checklists have proven invaluable.

Just as with other disciplines in which checklists are used, the stakes in nonviolent conflict are high. Those engaged in civil resistance are under profound stress as they risk life, property, and whatever slivers of freedom currently exist. The information that must be processed to make effective decisions can feel overwhelmingly complex. The Checklist will focus attention on critical long-term variables in the conflict and reduce reliance on less important, but often highly visible and emotional, short-term factors.

Students holding a sit-in at segregated lunch counters in Nashville, United States, 1960.

On this point, the surgeon and author Atul Gawande, who has researched the importance of checklists in a variety of contexts, writes that:

Checklists seem able to defend anyone, even the experienced, against failure in many more tasks than we realized. They provide a kind of cognitive net. They catch mental flaws inherent in all of us—flaws of memory and attention and thoroughness....[12]

Under conditions of true complexity—where the knowledge required exceeds that of any individual and unpredictably reigns... [effective checklists] ensure the stupid but critical stuff is not overlooked, and... ensure people talk and coordinate... to manage the nuances and unpredictabilities the best they know.[13]

The eight checklist questions are generic and should be relevant to any nonviolent conflict. Yet they should never be understood as or confused with a formula for success. Likewise, the Checklist cannot determine who will prevail, the dissident or the tyrant. However, it can offer a critical and continuing set of indicators to understand how citizen demands for freedom are (or are not) overcoming the entrenched power of tyrannical regimes.

The generic checklist questions will yield very specific answers that are based on the best information available that only local dissidents can know and that outsiders cannot necessarily fathom. In addition, depending on the details of the conflict, not all eight checklist questions will be equally significant at any given time, and the importance of moving a checklist answer from "no" to "yes" can rise or fall depending on the specific challenges posed by the tyrant.

The questions help to maximize a civil resistance campaign's probability of winning. They should invite careful consideration by individual dissidents as well as organized groups of pro-democracy activists. The answers can help to form a rallying cry to mobilize a population of millions of people. Maximizing the probability for this to occur is described in Chapter 5, "The Checklist Exercise for Freedom." The greatest value of this exercise is to create consensus among the people as to priorities for action. This reduces wasted energy and keeps expectations high. Meanwhile, the tyrant's hope for apathy and despair is crushed by a confident population.

---

12   Atul Gawande, *The Checklist Manifesto: How to Get Things Right* (New York: Picador, 2009), 47.
13   Gawande, 79.

Civil resistance strategies operate successfully in many different conflicts because tyrants depend on wide-scale obedience to remain in power. However, over time many citizens living under dictatorships refuse to remain apathetic forever.

Chapter Three

How Dissidents Build Capabilities

CHECKLIST QUESTION #1 | **Is the civil resistance campaign unifying around aspirations, leaders, and a strategy for winning?**

The primary attribute of successful civil resistance campaigns is unity. "Divide and rule" has long been the maxim of tyrants everywhere and throughout history. Those suffering under such conditions, to some degree, will have their unity fragmented. For most movements the internal challenge of discovering how to unify will determine when a campaign of civil resistance can begin to put a tyrant on the defensive.

Unity in a campaign of civil resistance has three dimensions:

- Aspirations
- Leadership
- Strategy

■ ASPIRATIONS

People living in a dictatorship have two choices: They can either wait passively in the hopes that a regime will evolve by itself to become more benign on its own, and in the meantime hang onto whatever remains of human value in a life lived under oppression, or they can mount an insurrection to dismantle the dictatorship using violent or nonviolent tactics.

For those choosing insurrection, a set of aspirations for a better life must be worthy of the risks of engaging in the conflict. These aspirations can be expressed as either "freedoms from" or "freedoms to."

"Freedoms from" are protections against the most dangerous features of tyranny, including incidents of violence, arbitrary detention, assets seizure, and the threats associated with each. "Freedoms to" are all the varied possibilities for human discovery and achievement, including uncensored speech, unrestricted travel, private entrepreneurship, and religious expression.

Among a range of population groups in society, there is likely to be a common interest in the "freedoms from" category. However, there is also likely to be divergences between types and intensities in the "freedoms to" category, as each individual, cultural, or religious group possesses its own aspirations for a better life. Finding a harmony among these aspirations is a precursor for high participation rates across genders, ages, ethnicities, economic status, and geography.

Unity of aspirations among pro-democracy activists does not require that the aspirations be strictly identified or that people's views are uniform. Diverse groups may not all be equally committed to a campaign of civil resistance, but to the degree they all support and participate to at least some extent, the more powerful their campaign will become.

The key is that what each dissident longs for in a post-tyrannical society is not in opposition to what their colleagues desire. The requirement is tolerance of one another's aspirations and not uniformity of those aspirations.

In the heat of a civil resistance campaign, people are expected to work with others they don't know well. If there is suspicion that some dissidents have hidden aspirations that threaten others, then the campaign will suffer. However, the successful execution of nonviolent tactics—that require shared risks and reliance on coordinated activity—will create increasing layers of trust and help allay any suspicion.

■ LEADERSHIP

Over the long-term, respecting a diversity of aspirations cannot be accomplished without trusted leadership that inspires confidence every day. A primary task for dissident leaders is to motivate diverse groups to support the common collective endeavor of civil resistance. To do this, leaders must satisfy the expectations of a population that the leader has a strategy that can triumph and justify the risks of waging nonviolent conflict.

What makes the task of unifying easier is that over time fewer and fewer citizens are exempt from a tyrant's cruelty and corruption, and so more and more will recognize the necessity of a major power realignment that requires a monumental fight with the tyrant, since no tyrant gives up power willingly.

While tyrants are adept practitioners of divide and rule, those who would challenge them must have leaders more skilled at fostering unity. This necessitates that movement leaders must have deep knowledge of the grievances and values of the diverse people that they wish to mobilize. Effective communication by leaders must resonate with the personal experience and feelings of ordinary people and summon their continued participation in nonviolent resistance even when prospects look bleak.

Unlike an army at war, campaigns of civil resistance do not have formal command and control authority over a mobilizing population. Therefore, tactical decisions must be organized and executed in

> *Tactical decisions must be organized and executed in ways citizens feel are commensurate with the risks they are willing to assume.*

ways citizens feel are commensurate with the risks they are willing to assume. A further complicating factor is that citizens with identical aspirations can have widely different tolerances for risk. Leaders must be aware of this dichotomy as well.

The leadership of each civil resistance campaign must discover their own way of operating. Some leadership styles will be more hierarchical, and others more decentralized. Most will feature a combination of both, reflecting different character traits of leadership within each civil resistance campaign. For every titular or charismatic national leader, there are many local leaders who need to be highly skillful at developing coalitions, negotiating, and aggregating interests among different groups on behalf of the whole. It is the ability of different leaders, on different scales (local or national), from different geographical parts of a country, representing different groups, to work together that will sustain unity over the long-term.

Each leadership style has its positive and negative aspects.

Gandhi's charismatic leadership was the only way to unite Hindus and Muslims against the British Raj. It also permitted Gandhi to unilaterally suspend the Salt campaign of 1930 when the British requested—as a condition of entering negotiations—that civil resistance be stopped. Gandhi then traveled to Lancaster, England, to negotiate with the British by himself. Indian National Congress leader Jawaharlal Nehru strongly advised against this and correctly predicted that Gandhi's suspension of operations would dissipate momentum and end the prospect of defections by the local police.

Unlike with Gandhi, the Green Movement in Iran and the pro-democracy movement in Hong Kong had the same amorphous leadership style and followed the same trajectories in the first few months. In both cases, the early power came from street protests largely generated spontaneously. Hong Kong dissidents advised resisters to "Be Water! We are formless. We are shapeless. We can flow. We can crash. We are like water!"[14]

There are two obvious advantages of this kind of amorphous leadership. First, the tyrant can't cut off the head of the campaign because it is impossible to find. Second, it is the spontaneity from this form of leadership that captures the energy emanating from an unexpected spark that can then ignite and propel the outrage of the entire population.

On the other hand, the problem with amorphous leadership is that it has trouble diversifying and sequencing tactical options. As the effectiveness of a single tactic such as mass protest diminishes (and it invariably will as tyrants refine their defenses), so too does confidence. Worse still, there may be no common voice against the use of violent tactics as protesters become increasingly frustrated and fearful.

The longer a nonviolent conflict unfolds, the greater the need for structured leadership. Otherwise, a campaign of civil resistance will degrade into random acts with diminishing effect.

Pro-democracy activists are far more likely to support coordinated leadership if they feel that those leaders are receptive to their best ideas. Successful campaigns will have an open communication loop whereby people across regions can provide continuous input to the leadership decisionmakers. Sustained continuity of effort and trust of each constituency in the other is key.

On the national level, it is not possible, nor necessarily advisable, for all of a movement's supporters to try to decide the movement's primary strategic direction. Conversely, it may not make sense for the most senior leadership to decide on specific tactics in a particular locality.

---

14 Mary Hui, Twitter post, June 25, 2019, 11:07 p.m.
    https://twitter.com/maryhui/status/1143717367521824768.

A civil resistance campaign should be designed to account for the environment, threats, opportunities, and capabilities of the various actors in the conflict. At the local level, no one will know these factors better than dissidents who live and organize themselves in these communities.

This grassroots level of influence creates opportunities and challenges for a campaign. It enables the campaign to act based on the most accurate information on the ground. But there remains no guarantee that these activists will make tactical decisions that align with a campaign's overall strategic objectives. This is a problem faced by all large organizations—whether governments, militaries, or businesses. However, unlike these other entities, campaigns of civil resistance cannot offer pay raises and promotions for obedience, nor dismissal or sanctions for disobedience. Civil resistance is after all a voluntary endeavor where outcomes can remain uncertain and dangerous for a protracted period of time. As such, civil resistance campaigns are dependent on intangible incentives to keep people united and guide them to act within a certain range of options that fall within a movement's broad plan for winning.

Most importantly, every people power movement is influenced by the culture of its citizens, including their preferences and norms in the arts, religion, ethnic customs, and social institutions. A movement's culture is incredibly important in impacting how a campaign of civil resistance can pressure the tyrant. Culture can incite teamwork, inclusivity, accountability, and discipline, paving the way for more high-quality strategic thinking rather than unreflective action. Movement culture is like DNA. It provides an imprint that makes it much easier for a nonviolent campaign to operate without a highly centralized command and control. Leaders must know how to leverage these proclivities for maximum participation.

■ STRATEGY

If unity requires inspiring leaders capable of addressing peoples' aspirations to end tyranny, then it also requires the glue of a widely understood and accepted theory of how to win.

With the incidence of nonviolent conflict accelerating in this century, it is even more important for pro-democracy activists to understand why people power succeeds or fails. Nonviolent conflict works across many different cases because it exploits two fundamental realities: first, that authoritarian regimes depend on

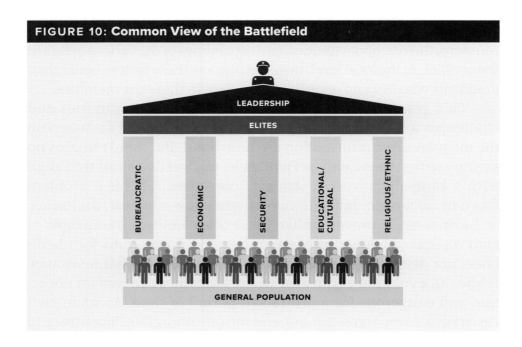

FIGURE 10: Common View of the Battlefield

LEADERSHIP

ELITES

BUREAUCRATIC

ECONOMIC

SECURITY

EDUCATIONAL/ CULTURAL

RELIGIOUS/ETHNIC

GENERAL POPULATION

wide-scale obedience among the populations they oppress in order to maintain their control, and second, that not everyone in dictatorships are equally determined to remain loyal through thick and thin. The battlefield illustrated in Figure 10 is identical to the battlefield presented in Chapter 2 to describe the risks of a strategy of violent insurrection.

The opportunity illustrated in Figure 11 has been described by Natan Sharansky, the iconic refusenik from the Russian gulags.

> *Every totalitarian society consists of three groups: true believers, double-thinkers and dissidents. In every totalitarian regime, no matter its cultural or geographical circumstances, the majority undergo a conversion over time from true belief in the revolutionary message into double-thinking. They no longer believe the regime but are too scared to say so. Then there are the dissidents—pioneers who dare to cross the line between double-thinking and everything that lies on the other side. In doing so, they first internalize, then articulate and finally act on the innermost feelings of the nation.*[15]

Double thinkers can move from "latent" to "revealed" and potentially become defectors themselves. A successful civil resistance

---

15   Natan Sharansky, "Street Smart," *Los Angeles Times*, June 26, 2009. https://www.latimes.com/archives/la-xpm-2009-jun-26-oe-sharansky26-story.html (accessed July 8, 2021).

= Latent double thinkers

LEADERSHIP CONTROL

campaign challenges a tyrant's demand for domestic tranquility and legitimacy. Through its many tactical encounters, it turns latent double thinkers (those who are sympathetic but unwilling to take risks, and therefore often hidden) into revealed double thinkers (those who become identifiable as people who are no longer fully loyal to the regime) and then into defectors (those who become known allies of the pro-democracy activists).

In Figure 12, tactics of civil resistance disrupt the status quo, and double thinkers move from latent to revealed. As this trend

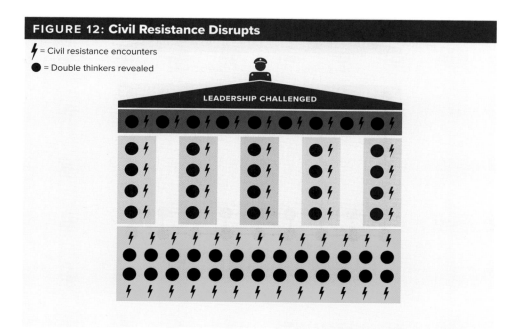

FIGURE 12: Civil Resistance Disrupts

= Civil resistance encounters

= Double thinkers revealed

LEADERSHIP CHALLENGED

accelerates it becomes more difficult for tyrants to maintain their aura of invincibility.

In Figure 13, civil resistance wins. Double thinkers proliferate and become more active, linking up with others who are like-minded. People become more visible about their disagreement with the tyrant, including siding openly with or joining the resistance campaign. As the linkages deepen and spread, the probability for defection increases at an even faster rate. Eventually the tyrant and his leadership base are set adrift, leading to a dramatic loss of legitimacy and influence. The result will either be the tyrant leaving outright or the opening of a negotiation for a new power sharing arrangement.

Nonviolent conflict succeeds when tactical disruptions accumulate to induce defections. There are an infinite variety of tactical options during every moment of a civil resistance campaign, which leaves many routes to victory. However, mindless selection of tactics without consideration of their impact will break down unity. People will not trust leaders who are operating without a continuous planning process that assesses how they are doing and how to adjust for weaknesses.

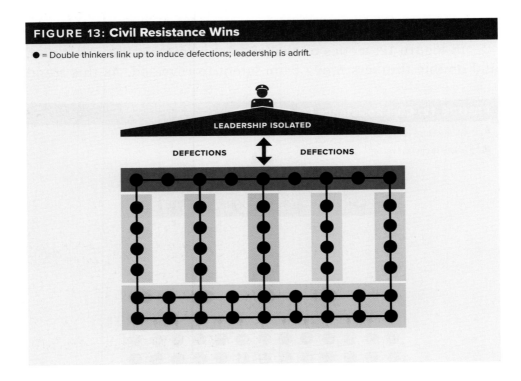

FIGURE 13: Civil Resistance Wins

● = Double thinkers link up to induce defections; leadership is adrift.

LEADERSHIP ISOLATED

DEFECTIONS   DEFECTIONS

With civil resistance as a superior alternative to violent insurrection, there can be no more consequential decision than how to confront the cruelty of a tyrannical regime. Getting that strategy wrong—as was the case in Syria in 2011 to the present day—can cost hundreds of thousands of lives and displace millions.[16]

CHECKLIST QUESTION #2 | Is the civil resistance campaign diversifying its tactical options while maintaining nonviolent discipline?

A tactic during a civil resistance campaign is conducted over a finite period of time and is designed to impose costs on a tyrant's system of command and control.

Tactical possibilities during a civil resistance campaign are only circumscribed by the imagination. The range is unlimited because tactical options emanate from how to undermine the tyrant's expectation of acceptable citizen behavior for all facets of a society. One caveat is that tactics with the intent to injure are excluded from nonviolent conflict. They are an integral part of a strategy of violent insurrection. Nonviolent tactics can augment violent strategies, but the reverse is not the case.

Gene Sharp's list of 198 methods was created fifty years ago during a simpler time. In today's increasingly complex and interdependent world, there are infinitely more opportunities to shut down normal commercial and social institutions that the tyrant expects to control. ICNC has published a list created by Michael Beer of 346 tactics that includes Sharp's 198 original tactics.[17]

What follows are 41 civil resistance campaigns that provide specific examples of nonviolent tactics.

---

16 See Maciej Bartkowski and Julia Taleb, "Myopia of the Syrian Struggle and Key Lessons," in *Is Authoritarianism Staging a Comeback?*, eds. Mathew J. Burrows and Maria J. Stephan (Washington, DC: Atlantic Council, 2015). https://www.nonviolent-conflict.org/wp-content/uploads/2016/01/Authoritarianism_Chapter10.pdf

17 Michael Beer, *Civil Resistance Tactics in the 21st Century* (Washington, DC: ICNC Press, 2021).

TABLE 7: 41 Civil Resistance Campaigns with Examples of Nonviolent Tactics

Nonviolent Campaign	Location	Years	Key Nonviolent Tactics
1. Revolution of Smiles against President Abdelaziz Bouteflika	Algeria	2019– 2020	Weekly protests and demonstrations; students' strikes (students boycott classes); general strike; women launched the "feminist square" for equal rights; workers' strikes and shutting down the transportation system; massive boycott of the presidential election
2. Anti-extradition and pro-autonomy campaign	Hong Kong	2019– 2020	Mass demonstrations, rallies; occupations of public spaces including university campuses and parks; general strike; labor strike; mass sit-ins at the Hong Kong International Airport; forming a 50km human chain called the "Hong Kong Way," inspired by the 1989 Baltic Way organized in three Baltic states during their nonviolent campaign for independence; election organizing that led to a landslide victory for a pro-democracy camp in the District Council election with a record high voter turnout in November 2019
3. Revolution against President Omar al-Bashir	Sudan	2018– 2019	Demonstrations; general strike; soldiers shielding protests against regime's security forces; protests to honor women who led the uprising; march to the headquarters of the armed forces; sit-ins; stay-in strikes
4. Women-led campaign against compulsory hijab	Iran	2018– 2019	Women standing on utility boxes and removing hijabs in public places; posting photos of their actions on social media; men joined the protest by reenacting similar actions and posting them on social media
5. Velvet Revolution	Armenia	2018	Protest walk through various towns and cities in Armenia; sit-in on the main square in the capital; mass marches; members of the Armed Forces of Armenia join the protests; blocking streets; workers' strike
6. "You Stink!" Campaign	Lebanon	2015– 2016	Chants protest; comical slogans; linking political figures to trash crisis; street protests in the capital
7. *Ficha Limpa* ("Clean Record") movement to enact anti-corruption bill	Brazil	2008– 2010	Sending regular alerts via social networks with calls for specific actions; online petition in support of the anti-corruption bill; email messaging and phone calls to legislators; e-petition memes; tweets; videos
8. Campaign in defense of the Anticorruption Commission	Indonesia	2009	Popular singers created anti-corruption songs; petitions; leafleting; hanging banners; sit-ins; gathering in front of the police station; concerts; street theater; public stunts; Happening art, such as "For a Healthy Indonesia, Fight Corruption" with a mass group exercise for the country's well- being
9. Campaign to curb police corruption	Uganda	2009– 2019	Developing a memorandum of understanding with law enforcement authorities about cooperation between anti-corruption campaign and police; community monitoring of police behavior; ethics training workshops with police integrity pledge signed at the end of the training; information gathering survey on whether people paid a bribe to the police in the last six months; meetings with residents about police codes of conduct and reporting police abuse and corruption

Nonviolent Campaign	Location	Years	Key Nonviolent Tactics
10. Democracy revolution against the absolutist monarchy	Nepal	2006	General regional and nationwide strikes (*bandhs*); marches; demonstrations; surrounding government buildings; mass protests; student-led protests and demonstrations
11. Social Audit Anti-Corruption Campaign	Kenya	2005	Holding community forums to educate people on public projects and their budgeting process; collecting input on community needs; gathering information on whether public projects were completed, their quality and costs; inspecting public projects; holding public hearings with residents and officials; puppet plays and using humor to ridicule and shame corruption and corrupt officials
12. *Shayfeen* ("We See You") anti-corruption campaign	Egypt	2005	Launching of the popular website shayfeen.com; logo of an eye, implying people watching the authority; distributing 100,000 tea glasses with the Shayfeen logo and a quarter of a million plastic bags for carrying bread with the slogan: "We see you, and at the elections we are observing you"; filming voting process and collecting evidence of fraud
13. Independence Intifada against Syrian troops in the country and the domination of state institutions	Lebanon	2005	Public funeral and funeral protests; rallies for "truth"; setting up a permanent protest encampment on the Martyr's square in the capital; voluntary contributions from people to sustain the tent encampment on the square; appropriating national anthem and national flag by nonviolent activists; no party flags were displayed; mass protests.
14. *Addiopizzo* ("Goodbye Protection Money") campaign against Mafia in Sicily	Italy	2004	Sticker campaign on lampposts in Palermo: "An entire people who pays *pizzo* is a people without dignity"; hanging out sheets with anti-mafia slogans on railings and bridges; at a soccer match unfurling a sheet "United against *Pizzo*"; collecting signatures of people who will buy at *pizzo*-free businesses; supporting owners that refused to pay *pizzo* by patronizing their stores; ethical consumerism action (patronizing *pizzo*-free businesses) that united businesses and customers against *pizzo*; distributing special stickers on windows of *pizzo*-free shops, *pizzo*-free yellow pages; *pizzo*-free product labeling; joint rallies and demonstrations; creating a sports team for the movement; supporting *pizzo*-free tourism; doing compliance checks to ensure businesses are being honest in their renunciation of doing business with the mafia
15. Nonviolent self-determination struggle by Western Saharans	Western Sahara	1999–2010	Student vigils; sit-ins in the city center; occupation of the symbolic square; displaying banned Saharawi flag; protest encampment just outside main city

Nonviolent Campaign	Location	Years	Key Nonviolent Tactics
16. Fifth Pillar anti-corruption campaign	India	2004–Present	Training people in how to file requests under the "right to information" law; refusal to pay bribes; public pledges against corruption; symbolic resistance (creation of the zero-rupee note as a way to show people were unwilling to pay for bribery); holding essay contests; human chains; sit-ins; flash public meetings; leafleting; signature collections; commemorations; community service in villages; theatre/performance; establishing a phone hotline for people to report corruption; posting accurate bureaucratic fees (for licenses, for example) publicly outside government offices so that people would know the legal cost of various services
17. Orange Revolution	Ukraine	2004–2005	Occupation of Maidan Square; tent encampment; social services organized to support the encampment; strikes; demonstrations; daily concerts; staged performances; reaching out to the security forces via retired military officials and international contacts; bring army to the side of the protesters; the army informed security forces loyal to the regime that they would protect protesters without arms
18. Women-led peace movement to end civil war	Liberia	2003	United group of Christian and Muslim women launched the campaign to end civil war; wearing all-white clothing symbolizing peace and gathering at the fish market every day for a week; sex strike to deny men intimacy until the war would end; organizing marches through the street of Monrovia; organized sit-ins in front of the building where peace negotiations were taking place in Accra, Ghana; threatening to disrobe and hold men in the building unless the peace agreement was signed
19. Blacklisting Corrupt Candidates	South Korea	2000	Launching a popular website featuring blacklisted political candidates; documentation about the unfit nominees and endorsements of uncorrupt candidates; getting candidate pledges to enact political reforms; promulgating a Peace Charter to instill nonviolent discipline during the protests; waiving yellow cards during rallies when names of blacklisted candidates were called out; organized the Red Festival where audience waived red cards and chanted "out"; candlelight rallies; signature drives; bicycle rally; farmers' convoys; children's protest; deploying shadow uncorrupt and respected candidates to 'shadow' blacklisted candidates
20. The Papuan Spring	West Papua	1999–2004	Creation of the Papuan parallel governing institutions; protests and demonstrations including by Papuan women market sellers; raising banned Papuan flag (Morning star)
21. Nonviolent campaign against President Slobodan Milosevic	Serbia	1998–2000	Rallies; marches; demonstrations; rock concerts; anti-Milosevic materials; strikes; boycotts; petitions; public statements; blocking of main roads; occupation of public spaces and buildings; street theatre and humorous skits with political and anti-Milosevic messages; opposition communicating with the security forces
22. One Minute of Darkness for Constant Light anti-corruption campaign	Turkey	1997	Each evening people would turn off their lights for one minute at the same time; banging pots and pans; flashlights; honking horns at intersections; candlelight vigils; neighborhood marches

Nonviolent Campaign	Location	Years	Key Nonviolent Tactics
23. March Revolution	Mali	1991	Using hereditary musicians called griots to disseminate information and stories about resistance; demonstrations; student strikes; march for peace
24. Civil resistance campaign	Kosovo	1989–1997	Establishment of parallel Albanian government and school system in Kosovo; protests; labor strikes; boycott of the Serbian-run schools and government institutions
25. Pro-democracy protest	China	1987–1989	Holding democratic salons; wall posters as a key communication strategy; posters; student petitions; student-led demonstrations; megaphoning residents with the information about the protests; school boycotts; open letters to the authorities; hunger strike occupation of Tiananmen Square
26. First Intifada	Palestine	1987–1993	Palestinian labor strikes; boycotts; parallel institutions; establishment of the joint Israeli–Palestinian committees
27. Solidarity Movement	Poland	1980s	Occupation of factories by workers; setting up independent professional associations; underground publications to break censorships; underground schooling; strikes; demonstrations; protests; resistance songs and humor
28. Anti-apartheid campaign	South Africa	1980s–1994	Boycotts of white-owned businesses in Port Elizabeth; civil disobedience of apartheid legislation and practices; public funeral processions; public declarations; multi-racial peace marches; kneeling marches; demonstrations; strikes and stay-aways; rent boycotts; school boycotts; sport and cultural event boycotts; international sanctions, divestment, and boycott campaign; creating alternative community-based institutions such as cooperatives, community clinics, legal resource centers
29. Struggle against military dictatorship	Chile	1985–1988	Labor strikes and labor slowdowns; church-based training in nonviolent resistance; demonstrations; singing; slowdowns in which people walked and drove slowly on a designated day; banging pots and pans; artistic protests; electoral organizing
30. People Power Revolution	Philippines	1983–1986	Candlelight vigils; rallies; demonstrations; electoral organizing; boycott of pro-regime media; school strikes; general strikes; mobilizing to protect nonviolent garrison of soldiers who defected from the regime; demonstrators greeting soldiers loyal to the regime with hugs and prayers
31. Resistance against Soviet invasion	Czechoslovakia	1968	Political non-cooperation; sit-ins; demonstrations; "Ten Commandments" of nonviolent resistance by Czechs and Slovaks against the Soviet troops published in the newspaper *Vecerni Prah* on August 26, 1968 — six days after the Soviet invasion. When a Soviet soldier approaches the local people for any type of assistance, the commandments called on people to do the following:

1. Don't know;
2. Don't care;
3. Don't tell;
4. Don't have;
5. Don't know how to;
6. Don't give;
7. Can't do;
8. Don't sell;
9. Don't show; and
10. Do nothing.

Nonviolent Campaign	Location	Years	Key Nonviolent Tactics
32. Nashville campaign in the US Civil Rights Movement	United States	1960	Activist trainings and drills in a church basement; lunch counter sit-ins; filling in jails; boycott of downtown businesses; mass march to the mayor's office
33. Positive Action independence campaign	Ghana	1949–1951	Economic boycotts against British goods, closing stores; sit-downs; establishment of independence schools
34. Bengali Language Movement	Bangladesh	1948–1952	General strike; funeral homages; establishment of language action committee and sociocultural organizations; strikes (International Mother Language Day was established by the UN in commemoration of this peaceful movement)
35. Nonviolent resistance against Nazi occupation	Denmark	1940–1944	"Ten Commandments" of Danish civil resistance that advocated and promoted working slowly, ineffectively, and badly for the Nazis; delaying or stopping transportation useful for Nazis; boycott German films and newspapers; boycott Nazis' stores; protect anyone that is pursued by Germans, which helped save 90 percent of the Danish Jews
36. Indian Independence Struggle	India	1930–1931	General civil disobedience against the British salt tax and monopoly on production and sale of salt; public statements and speeches by Gandhi and his supporters; mass petition; symbolic acts including public prayers and the display of a national Indian flag; singing; dancing; procession (the Salt March); public mourning of unarmed demonstrators killed by the British; economic boycott of British goods; *hartals* ("limited strikes"); school boycotts; occupation of salt depos; economic noncooperation and self-sustainability (homespun)
37. Egyptian Revolution of 1919 for independence from Britain	Egypt	1919–1921	Signature collection campaign in support of full independence; student strikes; workers' and peasants' strikes; women wore veils in protest; demonstrations at public funerals; boycott of British goods; mass prayer for independence; use of plays, music, and literature advocating disobedience
38. Persian Tobacco Protest	Iran	1890–1892	Boycott of tobacco products and nonviolent demonstrations against a British company's monopoly over the production, sale, and export of Persian tobacco
39. Resisting Russification in Russian Poland	Poland under partitions	1885–1914	Development of the Polish Flying University (Marie Curie, future first woman's Nobel laureate, graduated from this illegal university); boycott of the Russian state school system; launching of the Polish Motherland Schools
40. Passive Resistance campaign for equal political rights in the Habsburg Empire	Hungary	1850s–1860s	Refusal of military service; refusal to speak German socially; boycott of official celebrations; boycott of courts; boycott of Austrian goods; refusal to provide board and lodging for Austrian soldiers
41. Campaigns against the Stamp Act in the US colonies against the British crown	Britain's American Colonies	1765–1766	Nonimportation; boycotts; tax refusal; nonconsumption of British products

Despite the wide range of tactics employed in these 41 cases, they can be usefully categorized in two ways. First, nonviolent tactics can be categorized according to the risks taken by dissidents. *Tactics of concentration*, such as assemblies of protest or support, are high risk as they are big targets for violence by dictators. *Tactics of dispersion*, such as withdrawal from social institutions, are lower risk because they represent too many discrete and nonessential targets for violent repression.

Second, nonviolent tactics can also be categorized by the distinct ways in which a tyrant must respond. There are acts of commission, such as generalized strikes, in which the tyrant must coerce the dissidents into stopping what they are doing. There are also acts of omission, such as consumer boycotts of certain goods and services, that require a tyrant to induce dissidents to resume normal activity.

The most successful civil resistance campaigns use tactics from each of these categories. The reliance on any single tactic is not likely to constitute a winning strategy because not all citizens are willing to accept the same risks. Multiple tactics create a dilemma for the tyrant who will find it difficult to punish resistance while at the same time rewarding the cessation of disobedience.

> *Anyone who argues that a civil resistance campaign needs to be tolerant of allies who want to engage in violence is wrong.*

If access to many different tactics creates a strategic advantage for the resisters, then some may ask, "Why not add a discreet set of violent tactics into the mix?" This argument often arises when the nonviolent conflict seems to have temporarily lost momentum and frustration is growing. For this reason, all pro-democracy activists need to be convinced of the superiority of campaigns of civil resistance versus violent insurrection and must be prepared to argue and defend that point.

However, in some cases a civil resistance movement maintains commitment to nonviolent discipline but a violent group or insurgency arises outside the movement and begins to engage in violence alongside the movement. What then? Can this dynamic contribute to the nonviolent movement's chances of success?

Some argue yes because violent groups make pro-democracy activists seem reasonable and that the threat of violence scares the authorities into making concessions to more "moderate" civil resisters. However, this argument is not borne out by history. Scholars Erica Chenoweth and Kurt Schock conducted research on 106 nonviolent campaigns between 1900 and 2006 that sought a fundamental change in government.[18] In none of these cases could they find evidence of a positive effect for a civil resistance movement coexisting with active violent groups (which are sometimes referred to as "violent flanks"). Moreover, Chenoweth and Schock did find statistically significant evidence of the negative effects of interacting with a violent flank. For example, the average civil resistance movement with a violent flank was 17 percent smaller than the average civil resistance movement without a violent flank. Because high levels of civilian participation are a key factor leading to movement success, violent flanks indirectly reduce the chances to win the conflict.

Chenoweth and Schock also found that the presence of violent flanks strongly correlated with high levels of friction among dissidents. Mixing violent and nonviolent tactics diminishes a movement's prospects for remaining unified, thereby lowering the chances of winning. Violent flanks also increase the likelihood that pro-democracy activists will be more subject to repression, which depresses participation in the movement and thus further decreases its chances of success.

Chenoweth and Schock's findings of the incompatibility of violence and civil resistance are not surprising. Violent insurrections and civil resistance campaigns operate with completely contradictory dynamics. Even limited violence will damage the momentum needed to make a campaign of civil resistance effective. This is one reason why tyrants desperately try to provoke people to engage in violence or instigate violence through their use of *agents provocateurs* ("inciting agents").

Anyone who argues that a civil resistance campaign needs to be tolerant of allies who want to engage in violence is wrong. To go along with such a "big tent" argument functionally means that a civil resistance campaign should welcome into its midst forces that are alien to the idea of nonviolent conflict. Any reliance on allies willing to use violence will undermine the confidence and clarity that

---

18   Erica Chenoweth and Kurt Schock, "Do Contemporaneous Armed Challenges Affect the Outcomes of Mass Nonviolent Campaigns?," in *Mobilization: An International Quarterly* 20, no. 4 (2015): 427–451.

comes with maintaining nonviolent discipline. Disruption and defection of the tyrant's key supporters, which is key to success, is inhibited by the presence of violent insurrectionists. Common sense dictates that latent double thinkers will be unlikely to reveal themselves when they are being threatened with bodily harm or even death by the very people who desire them to defect to their side.

One question is whether or not sabotage should be viewed as a violent or nonviolent tactic. The answer is that it depends. Blowing up a train track just before a passenger train arrives is a violent tactic. But if the track is blown up and ample warning is given before a train passes, then it could be a nonviolent tactic. There is a bright line between the destruction of property and sabotage that poses a risk to human life, health, and physical well-being. Nowhere is that bright line easier to draw than when it comes to the taking down of surveillance infrastructure. Disabling cameras or infecting databases designed for social control with malware can hardly be considered violent. The tyrant may argue that these acts of sabotage are violent because they create disruption, but mass protests, strikes, and boycotts also create disruption to challenge the tyrant's legitimacy.

CHECKLIST QUESTION #3 | Is the civil resistance campaign sequencing tactics for maximum disruption with minimum risk?

Dissidents face the challenge of both choosing the right tactics and determining how they should be sequenced over time. The results of these choices are incredibly consequential. The average time frame of a successful nonviolent conflict is three years. To assume that there will be a short-term resolution of the conflict, and to deploy one tactic at a time without consideration for what comes next, can lead to failure.

To some intangible degree the impact of nonviolent tactics will be determined by the success or failure of prior nonviolent tactics. This explains why the same nonviolent tactic, implemented at different stages of a campaign, can produce very different pressures on the tyrant. A general strike in the early phases of a conflict can be premature but it could prove to be decisive at later phases. An illustration of this phenomenon is to contrast the events in Serbia in 2000 with those in China in 1989 and Venezuela in 2003.

In Serbia, strategically sequenced tactics against President Slobodan Milosevic resulted in his downfall in October 2000. The documentary *Bringing Down a Dictator* chronicled the major events of the battle to unseat Milosevic in what became known as the Bulldozer Revolution (after a memorable episode in which an engineering vehicle charged a state television building seen as Milosevic's propaganda stronghold). On October 5, 2000, many hundreds of thousands of protesters gathered in Belgrade.

But these events did not happen spontaneously. In fact, they were a culmination of strategically planned and sequenced campaign tactics that originated among groups in Serbian society. They began with irreverently humorous anti-regime activities and pranks led by the youth- and student-led group *Otpor!* ("Resistance!") that had been formed two years earlier. Over time the brutal regime went from being feared by the population to becoming its laughingstock. Otpor's trainings emphasized strategic planning, specific creative nonviolent actions and the absolute necessity of maintaining nonviolent discipline. The group played an important role in unifying divided opposition and launched the *Gotov je!* ("He is finished!") campaign leading up to the September 2000 presidential elections. Activists distributed more than two million stickers with the *Gotov je!* slogan and spread anti-regime graffiti around the country. The opposition also reached out to the police and the military to shift their allegiance in favor of the resistance. When Milosevic attempted to steal the elections, the population was ready.

Three days after the elections on September 27, 2000, Milosevic falsely claimed that Kostunica had not earned a majority and was therefore subject to a runoff election with him. Nonviolent demonstrations then began with walkouts by school students, which spread to strikes demanding Milosevic to stand down. Other worker groups soon joined the striking miners in the Kolubara region, which produced most of the country's electricity. This led to a general strike of the Serbian population with transport workers blocking key highways and main roads. The strike paralyzed cities and towns across the country and spread the regime forces thin. On October 4, strike supporters prevented police that remained loyal to the regime from breaking the Kolubara strike while the opposition issued the ultimatum to Milosevic to step down. On October 5, it was estimated that up to one million people descended on the streets of

Belgrade from around the country and joined a nonviolent mass rally in the capital. A day later, when it was clear the police would no longer side with the regime, Milosevic acknowledged electoral defeat and surrendered.

A primary reason why civil resistance campaigns have experienced major failures is because of the inability to sequence a diverse array of nonviolent tactics into a coherent strategic plan. Without such a plan the probability of mass mobilization capable of spreading over a country is much diminished. The lessons of the Tiananmen protests in 1989 and the general strike in Venezuela in 2002–2003 are telling examples.

Chinese pro-democracy students concentrated their single tactic of street protests in many cities but most notably in the capital. Only symbolically powerful, this geographic concentration of opposition force provided the regime with greater opportunity to isolate them. The tyrant could cut their communication to other cities and regions, physically encircle their protests, and initiate brutal and swift crackdowns by its loyal armed forces. At the same time, state propaganda depicted students in the capital as terrorists and violent usurpers. In retrospect, the civil resistance campaign dissipated whatever momentum it might have had by failing to diversify its tactics and execute them outside of Beijing.

Civil resistance campaigns fail due to the inability to sequence a diverse array of nonviolent tactics into a coherent strategic plan.

In the case of Venezuela, the political opposition launched a strike in 2002 to force then President Hugo Chavez to hold a new presidential election. The strike, led by business and trade union federations, lasted three months and ended in failure. Private television networks provided daily and unrestricted coverage of the strike, helping to sustain its momentum. The strike initially led to the stoppage at the major state oil company but also produced divisions among the public. The action failed to win support among ordinary Venezuelans and many business owners chose not to join. Chavez also mobilized his supporters and organized large pro-government and anti-strike rallies blaming strikers for shortages of gasoline and basic foods that impacted Venezuelans.

In a counterattack (not unlike what happened in Hong Kong in 2020), the Venezuelan government began to fire striking executives, managers, and workers and to bring in strikebreakers consisting of loyal employees to restart work. The pressure from the regime to end the strike increased as more small and medium businesses that initially joined the strike re-opened to avoid bankruptcy while the government propaganda continued to mobilize the public against the strikers. The military's loyalty to Chavez remained strong and the regime was able to deploy repressive measures, including the firing of thousands of strikers and targeted arrests, that eventually suppressed the strike.

In the essay "The Future of Nonviolent Resistance," Chenoweth explains the different outcomes between Serbia, China, and Venezuela by offering advice to today's pro-democracy activist:

> ...movements that engage in careful planning, organization, training, and coalition-building prior to mass mobilization are more likely to draw a large and diverse following than movements that take to the streets before hashing out a political program and strategy.[19]

In her essay, Chenoweth goes on to point out two contradictory trends in civil resistance during this century: the dramatic acceleration of cases of nonviolent conflict and the substantial reduction in success rates of those conflicts. This can be explained because fewer are unfolding like Serbia, where the momentum was with the dissidents, and more are unfolding like China and Venezuela where the momentum was with the tyrants.

To maintain momentum, dissidents must prioritize tactics that:

- Strengthen the relationship between societal disruption and defection of those on whom the tyrant most depends; and

- Weaken the relationship between repression and obedience on which the tyrant relies to maintain order.

These relationships are illustrated in Figure 14. The upper right quadrant describes the dissident's terrain. It is the dissident's task to prioritize tactics so they will move along Line A with minimal levels of societal disruptions creating the maximum number of defections from the tyrant. The tyrant wants to reduce the efficiency of dissidents' tactics as seen on Line B, where even high levels of disruption through nonviolent tactics lead to fewer defections. If the

---

19 Erica Chenoweth, "The Future of Nonviolent Resistance," in *Journal of Democracy* 31, no. 3 (July 2020): 69–84.

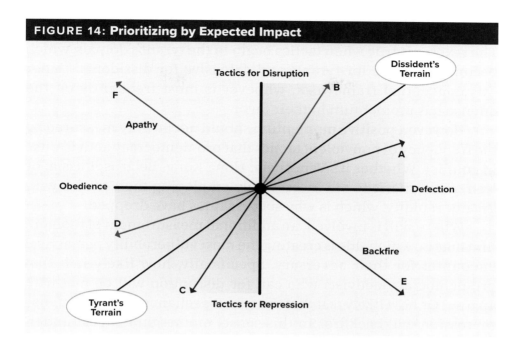

FIGURE 14: Prioritizing by Expected Impact

tyrant's efforts in keeping the pro-democracy activist moving along Line B are successful, then eventually societal disruption will yield no defections and render the opposition apathetic as expressed by Line F.

The bottom left quadrant describes the tyrant's terrain. The tyrant aspires to use minimal levels of violent repression to extract the most obedience from citizens (Line D). In contrast, the civil resistance campaign benefits when the tyrant believes he has to rely on maximum levels of violent repression—necessitating the use of considerable resources and diminishing political legitimacy—to extract minimal levels of societal obedience (Line C). When an increase in the intensity and scale of repression yields no obedience but only defections, then the repression is backfiring (Line E).

Nonviolent conflict is the sum of tactical encounters occurring on the dissident's terrain and on the tyrant's terrain. The more frequently the outcomes of these encounters fall along the green lines, the more likely the dissident has superior skills. When the outcomes track the orange lines, that may reflect the superior skills of the tyrants.

Momentum in every competition is hard to define but palpable to the contestants striving to win. One way to measure momentum in a nonviolent conflict is to base it on who is initiating the most tactical encounters. Tactics which are initiated in the dissident's terrain are offensive for dissidents and defensive for tyrants. The reverse is true when tactics begin in the tyrant's domain which become offensive for tyrants and defensive for dissidents. Under this conceptual framework, whoever is most frequently on the offense has momentum in their favor.

However, positive momentum should not be fully measured by the frequency of nonviolent tactics that pro-democracy activists use in conflict. Whether it's Venezuela, Hong Kong, Belarus, Russia, or Iran, authoritarians are increasingly employing their tactics with greater rapidity, which is why success rates have dropped.

Where skill is involved, an additional measurement of momentum may be which side is creating the most vulnerability per tactical encounter for their adversary. Specifically, how likely is it that pro-democracy activists who call for disruption will be met with apathy? Or how likely is it that the tyrant's reliance on more intense repression will backfire? In this sense, momentum is best understood by relative changes in levels of vulnerability between the dissident and the tyrant.

At every point in the nonviolent conflict, it is important to assess whether the civil resistance campaign is likely to degrade into apathy before the tyrant's repression backfires. The best protection against apathy is to expand the variety of tactical encounters so there is always some confrontation, big or small, that puts tyrants on their heels. The best way to create backfire is to have the tyrant invest in violence that fails to coerce.

When choosing tactics and how to sequence them, dissidents should consider an innovative dimension which involves the use of credible threats of nonviolent action. Every tactic in a nonviolent conflict can be a source of short-term direct pressure or long-term indirect pressure, or both. A tyrant normally has a history of using violence, so when the regime threatens to use violence, the population assumes the threat has a real possibility of occurring. But there is no instant believability that comes with the threat of nonviolent action because it is unlikely that dissidents from a specific nonviolent conflict have any prior history of implementing similar tactics. A threat by dissidents to use a tactic—for example, a boycott—for the first time may not be believed.

One exception to this is mass protests, the tactic which occurs most frequently during nonviolent conflicts. In a recent article,

"The Power of Words: State Reactions to Protest Announcements," Johannes Vüllers and Elisa Schwarz note:

> Organizations often announce their protest activities prior to their implementation to mobilize awareness, recruit supporters, and receive media attention.[20]

> Facing a protest announcement, the government has three different options: (a) ignoring the announcement, (b) taking preventive measures to ensure the protest will not be implemented, or (c) providing concessions to prevent the protest from taking place.[21]

If the tyrant refuses to accept the risk of ignoring the protest announcement and does not take preventative measures, then the tyrant is forced to provide concessions. This immediately gives pro-democracy activists leverage because latent double thinkers will become aware of the tyrant's discomfort and reluctance to use force.

Now imagine if such opportunities to threaten the tyrant extended to other nonviolent tactics including strikes, boycotts, and numerous other tactics of commission and omission.

To make any particular tactic a credible threat it would need to have been implemented before with sufficient power that the tyrant would negotiate to avoid its next use.

One particularly effective tactic used by the Hong Kong dissidents was their occupation of the airport for three days in August 2019. As a result of their success in shutting down the Hong Kong International Airport, they could subsequently threaten to execute an airport sit-in any time they might choose. They could both start and finish the occupation under their own terms. While maintaining nonviolent discipline, Hong Kong's pro-democracy activists could sequence other tactics that could be turned on and off and then threatened.

CHECKLIST QUESTION #4 | Is the civil resistance campaign discovering ways to make external support more valuable?

Too often dissidents feel the missing link to their success is external support. The most common manifestation of this is the desperate desire for the world's recognition of their plight.

---

20 Johannes Vüllers and Elisa Schwarz, "The Power of Words: State Reaction to Protest Announcements," *Comparative Political Studies 52*, no. 3 (2019): 347.

21 Vüllers and Schwarz, "The Power of Words," 353.

Erica Chenoweth and Maria Stephan's groundbreaking study *The Role of External Support in Nonviolent Campaigns: Poisoned Chalice or Holy Grail?* systematically evaluates the effects of external assistance on maximalist nonviolent conflicts (i.e., those seeking to effect regime change). Chenoweth and Stephan recognize the ubiquity of external actors in twenty-first century nonviolent conflict and how they can help "generate high participation, maintain nonviolent discipline, deter crackdowns, and elicit security force defections."[22] At the same time, they reject the notion that civil resistance campaigns must rely on outside assistance to avoid failure.

The study is the first of its kind. All prior studies have focused more generally on external assistance to social movements in a democratic or semi-democratic context, or on external assistance to armed rebellions directly challenging the authority of tyrants.

The quantitative part of the study includes the analysis of original data collected from 25,000 publicly reported incidents of external assistance to 68 maximalist nonviolent campaigns operating worldwide: 67 campaigns from 2000 to 2014 and one historical case (South Africa) outside of that time period.

The qualitative part of Chenoweth and Stephan's study includes eighty interviews with key stakeholders, donors, policymakers, journalists, human rights advocates, and others covering eight campaigns.

By integrating these qualitative and quantitative data, the study reviews:

- Timing of Assistance (see Table 8)
- Types of Support (see Table 9)
- Types of Supporters (see Table 10)
- Types of Recipients (see Table 11)

Tables 8–11 organize the data to demonstrate how external assistance can "sustain high participation, maintain nonviolent discipline, deter crackdowns and elicit defections."[23]

---

22 Erica Chenoweth and Maria J. Stephan, *The Role of External Support in Nonviolent Campaigns: Poisoned Chalice or Holy Grail?* (Washington, DC: ICNC Press, 2021), 1.

23 Chenoweth and Stephan, *The Role of External Support,* 18.

FIGURE 15: Eight Histories of Early 21st Century Campaigns

Belarus
2006
Denim Revolution

Ukraine
2004–2005
Orange Revolution

Serbia
2000
Bulldozer
Revolution

Tunisia
2010–2011
Jasmine
Revolution

Egypt
2011
January 25
Revolution

Syria
2011–2013
Syrian Uprising

Iran
2009
Green Revolution
and Day of Rage

Sudan
2011–2013
Anti-al-Bashir
Revolution

TABLE 8: Timing of Assistance

■ **Pre-Campaign:** Incidents of external assistance that began in the five years before the campaign commenced. For instance, providing financial assistance to media organizations to protect press freedom, training workshops for student activists, or computers or cell phones to poll workers prior to elections.

■ **Peak Campaign:** Incidents of external assistance that began during the period of mass mobilization—i.e., while there were at least 1,000 observed participants mobilized continuously as part of the maximalist campaign.

For instance, small grants to civil society groups advocating for civil rights, legal aid for human rights defenders who are imprisoned, or diplomatic maneuvers to express support and solidarity for the opposition.

■ **Post-Campaign:** Incidents of external assistance that began during the two-year period after the campaign ended, either in success (i.e., the removal of the incumbent national leader or territorial independence) or failure (i.e., the demobilization of the campaign, below 1,000 observed participants). For instance, mediating dialogue sessions regarding constitutional reforms, providing economic relief to support democratic reforms, or calling for transitional justice processes.

■ **Financial** Direct monetary assistance (e.g., small or large grants, scholarships, cash, loans, strike funds, legal funds, food, medicine, debt relief, etc.). *Example: Finland dedicates $13,236 USD for democratic participation and civil society to support Indian representation within Mexican democracy, 1997–2001 (pre-campaign support, anti-Calderon movement, Mexico).*

■ **Moral / symbolic** Nonviolent solidarity actions (e.g., digital campaigning or advocacy, mobilization on behalf of group in one's own country, showcasing activist cause and work, providing awards, visiting the country, directly participating in the campaign in the country, like US Ambassador Robert Ford marching with Syrians in July 2011). *Example: Amnesty International issued a public appeal for letters of support on behalf of two men who had not been seen since they were taken into custody during election protests, 18 August 2000 (peak campaign support, anti-Fujimori campaign, Peru).*

■ **Technical** Assistance with planning, logistics, intelligence, coordination, convening activists, conducting and delivering background research, and the implementation of campaign-related tasks (e.g., putting activists in touch with one another, providing warnings of impending repression, providing physical space for training and organization without necessarily conducting the training, and providing a strategic analysis of the situation, providing direct legal assistance, providing direct medical assistance). Provision of equipment (e.g., cell phones, computers, cameras), printing, books and articles, translations. Relationship-building or convening for the purpose of relationship-building. *Example: The British government commits £800,000 GBP to develop an independent media center in Ukraine to cooperate and train journalists, politicians, businesses, layers, judges, and NGO leaders, 2002–2005 (peak campaign support, Orange Revolution, Ukraine).*

■ **Training** The provision of leadership training, organizational capacity-building, labor organizing, movement training, legal training, medical training. Note that this category explicitly requires the supporter to train the activists (not just provide space for training, which is coded as technical support). *Example: The Slovak Academic Information Agency and Freedom House held a seminar in March 1999 in Bratislava, featuring the leaders of the OK'98 campaign and 35 participants from Ukraine, Croatia, Serbia, Belarus, Russia, Kyrgyzstan, the Caucasus, and Lithuania. The goal of the seminar was to make the participants familiar with the experience of Slovak CSOs in increasing citizens' involvement in public affairs. The seminar was designed mostly for attendants from Croatia and Yugoslavia, countries that were still struggling with authoritarian regimes and that could make the best use of Slovakia's experience, 1999 (pre-campaign support, Bulldozer Revolution, Serbia).*

■ **Nonviolent civilian protection** Protective accompaniment, nonviolent inter-positioning, monitoring, mediation between conflict participants, monitoring regime behavior, ceasefires, and other local conditions. *Example: The Committee to Protect Journalists released a report detailing the first-ever deaths of Syrian journalists by the government and expressed outrage, 2012 (peak campaign support, Syrian Uprising).*

■ **Sanctions against regime** Issuing active sanctions (e.g., tangible bilateral or multilateral penalties) in direct response to regime's actions toward the campaign. Includes travel bans, exclusion from meetings, freezing assets, imposing arms embargoes, or other measures (e.g., multinational corporations withdrawing from South Africa in opposition to apartheid, etc.). *Example: In Melbourne, union-ists held South African engineering goods as a virtual ransom for the release of trade unionists in South Africa, 1985 (peak campaign support, anti-Apartheid campaign, South Africa).*

■ **Safe passage for defectors** Providing asylum, amnesty, golden parachutes, or other incentives for regime elites to concede to the campaign or leave the country. *Example: The presidents of the US, Kazakhstan, and Russia jointly negotiated for Interim President Kurmanbek Bakiyev to step down, 2010 (peak campaign support, anti-Interim Government campaign, Kyrgyzstan).*

■ **Preventing / mitigating repression** Providing safe havens for activists, grant-ing asylum or refugee status to activists, demanding activist release from prison, calling out or issuing démarches in response to abuses of activists, issuing indict-ments, arresting and trying war criminals, etc.), blocking or stalling on military aid shipments. *Example: The Indian government expressed concern about the crackdown on pro-democracy protesters by the Gayoom regime, 2003–2008 (peak campaign support, anti-Gayoom campaign, Maldives).*

■ **Removal of support** An ally withdrew tangible support for the opponent gov-ernment (e.g., US President Reagan threatening to reduce aid to the Philippines under Marcos, the US withholding aid from Egypt in mid-2013). *Example: France recalled its Ambassador, announced that it would block new investment in South Africa, and said it would introduce a resolution in the UN Security Council con-demning South Africa for its apartheid policies of racial segregation and urging concerted international action against it, 1985 (peal campaign support, anti-apartheid movement, South Africa).*

■ **International nongovernmental organization (INGO)** Formal, private organization that undertakes activities to assist people in other countries. Can include advocacy organizations (e.g., Amnesty International, Human Rights Watch, Nonviolent Peaceforce, International Fellowship of Reconciliation), foundations and philanthropic organizations (e.g., Open Society, International Center on Nonviolent Conflict, Nonviolence International), humanitarian organizations (e.g., International Red Cross and Red Crescent), educational or training groups (e.g., CANVAS, Rhize), and adjuncts to religious groups (e.g., Catholic Relief Services). *Examples: Amnesty International, Human Rights Watch, Maldives Election Watch, National Democratic Institute, International Republican Institute, Committee to Protect Journalists.*

■ **Diaspora group** A collection of people living abroad who engage in advocacy on behalf of people living in their home countries (e.g., Tamils in Canada, Sudanese in the United States). *Examples: Lebanese in Kuwait, Syrian expats in Jordan, Malawi Diaspora Forum.*

■ **University / student group** Formal or informal groups of students, educators and intellectuals who engage in advocacy (e.g., Indonesian students advocating on behalf of Timorese activists). *Examples: McGill University students, Harvard University students, DC Coalition against Apartheid and Racism, Iranian students from multiple universities.*

■ **Transnational solidarity network (TAN)** Formal or informal collections of activists who mobilize in support of struggles in other countries. Often (but not always) involves groups in the Global North mobilizing on behalf of groups in the Global South (e.g., American celebrities mobilizing in support of the anti-Apartheid movement in South Africa). Includes external movements (e.g., Egyptian April 6 activists who sent pizza to Wisconsin labor activists in 2011). Excludes transnational unions or organized labor groups, which are coded separately (see below). *Examples: Canadian Election Observers, American Committee on Africa, Tunisian Association of Democratic Women, FEMEN.*

■ **Individual** A person acting in her/his individual capacity (e.g., a Nobel Peace Prize Laureate, celebrity advocate, a financier). Excludes people acting as part of their roles in an organized group in any other category. *Examples: Dalai Lama, Desmond Tutu, Elie Wiesel, Betty Williams.*

■ **International governmental organization (IGO)** A multilateral governmental organization, such as the United Nations, World Bank, International Labor Organization, or International Criminal Court. Includes regional IGOs such as the European Union. *Examples: UNICEF, UNDP, OSCE, NATO, EC, World Bank, IMF.*

■ **Corporation** A company or firm. Typically, a multinational corporation, such as Shell Oil, General Motors, AT&T, or Nike. *Examples: Barclays, Motorola, Twitter, DigitalGlobe, Columbia Pictures, Google Ideas.*

■ **Foreign government** A foreign government (e.g., the United States Government), an agency within a government (e.g., the US State Department), or an individual acting on behalf of a government (e.g., the US Secretary of State). *Examples: US, Germany, Spain, Netherlands, Norway, Sweden, Russia, France, India.*

■ **Transnational labor organization / union** A transnational non-governmental labor group (e.g., the AFL-CIO). Excludes the International Labor Organization, which is an IGO. *Examples: The Operative Painters and Decorators Union, Central Council of Trade Unions of Czechoslovakia, AFL-CIO, Congress of South African Trade Unions (COSATU), International Trade Union Confederation, Solidarity Center.*

■ **Rebel / paramilitary / militia group** An armed non-state or semi-state actor from within or without the country (e.g., Vietnamese insurgents giving advice to South Africa anti-apartheid activists). *Examples: Hamas, Hezbollah, FARC.*

■ **Media** A formal or informal media organization providing direct coverage of the movement. *Examples: Omroep voor Radio Freedom (Broadcasters for Radio Freedom), Pan African News Agency, The Guardian, Morning Star, Democratic Voice of Burma.*

■ **Civil society organization (CSO)** Formal civil society organizations. Can include local or transnational advocacy organizations (e.g., Amnesty International, Human Rights Watch, Nonviolent Peaceforce, International Fellowship of Reconciliation), foundations and philanthropic organizations (e.g., Open Society, International Center on Nonviolent Conflict, Nonviolence International), humanitarian organizations (e.g., International Red Cross and Red Crescent), educational or training groups (e.g., CANVAS, Rhize), and religious groups and institutions (e.g., Catholic Relief Services). Can include state-run or independent CSOs. *Examples: Zambian NGOs, Association of Independent Electronic Media, Center for Free Elections and Democracy, Izlaz 2000, Lebanese Red Cross.*

■ **University / student group** Formal or informal groups of students, educators and intellectuals who engage in advocacy (e.g., Indonesian students advocating for human rights). *Examples: Togo student groups, Students from UNESCO Project Schools, University Graduates of Tunisia, Haitian youth groups.*

■ **Individual** A person acting in her/his individual capacity (e.g., a Nobel Peace Prize Laureate, celebrity advocate, a financier). Excludes people acting as part of their roles in an organized group in any other category. *Examples: Blogger Win Zaw Naing, Zarganar (Burma's most famous comedian), former Prime Minister Abd Al-Karim Al-Iryani, a UNDP Beirut intern, unspecified individuals.*

■ **Business or corporation** A local company or firm. Typically, small- and medium-sized enterprises located in the country in which the movement is involved. Can be state-owned or independent. *Examples: South African black businessmen, Tunisian Dairy Sector, Ukrainian Telekritika.*

■ **Government** Governments or elements of the government (e.g., the Egyptian Government), an agency within a government (e.g., the Egyptian military), or an individual acting on behalf of a government (e.g., the chief of staff of the Egyptian military). *Examples: Thai government, Nepalese government, Belarus government.*

■ **Labor organization / union** Organized labor groups (e.g., unions). Can be state-owned or independent. *Examples: Independent Media Trade Union of Ukraine and the National Union of the Journalists of Ukraine, Bolivian Labor Party, Belarusian labor unions, South African Congress of Trade Unions.*

■ **Rebel / paramilitary / militia group** An armed non-state or semi-state actor from within or without the country (e.g., Vietnamese insurgents giving advice to South Africa anti-apartheid activists). *Examples: Sudan Revolutionary Front, Polisario Front, West Papuan rebels.*

■ **Local media** A formal or informal media organization providing direct coverage of the movement. Can be state-owned or independent. *Examples: Charter-97, Radi B92, Association for Independent Electronic Media (ANEM), Lebanese Broadcasting Corporation.*

■ **Formal opposition parties** Legal opposition political parties operating in the country. *Examples: Zajedno Coalition, African National Congress, Maoist Party of Nepal, Sudanese Congress Party, Awami League.*

■ **Movement activists** Civilians, including activists, movement leaders, and grassroots groups who receive direct assistance outside of the context of any of the categories above. *Examples: movement activists in South Africa, Zambia, Ukraine, Tunisia, Yemen, Egypt, Iran.*

■ **Unspecified** There is evidence of support, but the available information regarding the support is too general to specify the recipient. *Examples: Unspecified public recipients in Syria, Morocco, Mauritania, Togo, Tunisia, Ukraine, South Africa, Lebanon, Burma, Thailand.*

■ **Other** All others not listed here. *Examples: Zambian traditional leaders, Local minority groups in Serbia, Lakas Community in the Philippines, relatives of Gas War Victims in Bolivia, Thai women leaders.*

This extraordinary encyclopedia of information allows pro-democracy activists to identify comprehensively and with precision the most promising opportunities for external assistance. Based on their findings, Chenoweth and Stephan offer nine general observations:

- *Few nonviolent uprisings in the past twenty years existed without significant international attention and involvement....*

- *Long-term investment in civil society and democratic institutions can strengthen the societal foundations for nonviolent movements....*

- *Activists who receive training prior to peak mobilization are much more likely to mobilize campaigns with high numbers, low fatalities, and greater likelihood of defections. Training provides important skills-building functions, but perhaps even more importantly, it can provide direct avenues for relationship-building, peer learning, and spaces for strategic planning.*

- *Mitigating regime repression via political, diplomatic, and security engagement is a critical form of assistance that supports an enabling environment for nonviolent organizing and mobilizing....*

- *Generally speaking, support from foreign governments appears to indirectly help most campaigns. But this finding does not mean that direct government assistance helps movements win....*

- *Concurrent external support to armed groups tends to undermine nonviolent movements in numerous ways....*

- *Repressive regimes often benefit from outside support from powerful allies, posing a significant challenge for activists....*

- *Direct funding to movements has few effects on movement characteristics or outcomes.... Flexible donor funding that minimizes bureaucratic obstacles has been most helpful to movements.*

- *Donor coordination is important to be able to effectively support and leverage nonviolent campaigns.... This insight helps us understand not just the* who *and* what *of external assistance, but also the* how. *Unity and cohesion are important for movements and donors alike....*[24]

---

24 Chenoweth and Stephan, *The Role of External Support*, 1–3.

*Anti-Marcos farmers protest during the People Power
Movement in the Philippines, 1986.*

While this study affirms the many opportunities to capitalize on the availability of outside assistance, there are caveats with every form of intervention except one: "training seems to effectively support nonviolent campaigns more consistently than any other form of assistance."[25]

It is clear that in order for new and old tyrants of the world to "retire," pro-democracy activists must become more competitive. There are no negative effects of training as many dissidents as humanly possible. This transfer of knowledge to hundreds of thousands of key pro-democracy activists can provide one of the greatest opportunities for all humanity to undermine tyranny. This should be the focus of worldwide efforts—particularly from private, foundational support.

---

25 Ibid., 5.

When it comes to measuring the resilience of a civil resistance campaign, numbers matter the most. Tyrants are well aware that more campaign participants will reduce the impact of their violent repression and therefore their capacity to control the population they currently govern.

Chapter Four

How Dissidents Navigate Conflict

CHECKLIST QUESTION #5 | **Are the number and diversity of citizens confronting the tyranny likely to grow?**

The rate of civilian participation is one of the most important trends for movement leaders to monitor and stimulate over the course of a nonviolent conflict. The changing numbers and diversity of people engaging in civil resistance is a barometer of whether momentum favors the tyrant or the dissident.

When it comes to measuring the resilience of a movement, numbers matter the most. Tyrants are well aware that the more participants in civil resistance efforts, the less impactful will be their use of violent repression and the less likely they will be able to maintain control over the population.

As a campaign's support base expands to include new groups with unique skills, opportunities, and resources, it can diversify its tactics by opening new fronts against the tyrant. For example, factory workers may go on strike (first front), and later be joined by miners who also stop working (second front). Students can boycott classes (third front). Farmers can disrupt the food supply chain on a geographically dispersed basis (fourth front). More and more new tactics on additional fronts (e.g., healthcare facilities and sporting events) may be incorporated as the conflict progresses. Each cadre of civil resisters has their own networks and assets while the tyrant has to stretch his resources thinner and thinner to try to secure access denied him in different spaces and times.

Just as groups can deny the dictator access to their networks and assets, so too can they offer these capabilities to a growing civil resistance campaign. One way this can manifest is when a movement's supporters work together to create parallel social, economic, and political structures as an alternative to the regime's oppressive status quo. As participation increases, these alternative institutions become bases for a movement's power and resilience, and they can play a critical role in stabilizing and consolidating the gains made by the movement, especially as it closes in on a democratic transition.[26]

High rates of civilian participation also increase the probability of defections from the tyrant's pillars of support. The more people who join a campaign, the more connections the campaign has to its opponent's key supporters. Civil servants, politicians, members of the security forces, businessmen who are benefitting from the regime, members of the judiciary, and journalists who work for state media may all know people who participate in nonviolent conflict. Their attitudes are influenced by the people around them who may shame them for profiting from the dictatorship. The more their family members, friends, colleagues, religious authorities, and others they care about are sympathetic to the campaign and critical of the tyrant, the greater likelihood of a shift in their loyalties.

One category of participants requires special attention, namely, the role of women in civil resistance. Women have been more important in past campaigns then generally recognized. Between 1949 and 2013, there were at least 95 nonviolent campaigns with women's frontline participation that succeeded against a militarily more powerful foreign occupier, colonizer, or repressive domestic regime (see Table 12). The Women in Resistance (WiRe) dataset has shown that "women's participation is highly correlated with successful resistance campaigns."[27] Women's involvement increases levels of public participation, heightens the prospects of defections from the military, and improves the likelihood of maintaining nonviolent discipline. Indeed, lack of women's frontline participation makes civil resistance 24 percent more likely to fail.[28]

---

26 See also Maciej Bartkowski, "Alternative Institution-Building as Civil Resistance," *Minds of the Movement*, posted June 13, 2018. https://www.nonviolent-conflict.org/blog_post/alternative-institution-building-civil-resistance/.

27 Erica Chenoweth, Conor Seyle, and Sahana Dharmapuri, *Women's Participation and the Fate of Nonviolent Campaigns: A Report on the Women in Resistance (WIRE) Data Set* (Policy Brief). Broomfield, CO: One Earth Future, October 2019. https://www.oneearthfuture.org/file/1964/download?token=VUcOhryR.

28 Ibid.

TABLE 12: 95 Successful Civil Resistance Campaigns with Significant Women's Frontline Participation Against Foreign or Domestic Tyrannies Between 1949–2013[29]

Campaign	Location	Start	End	Target
Convention People's Party movement	Ghana	1949	1957	British rule
Anti-Jimenez campaign	Venezuela	1958	1958	Jimenez dictatorship
April Revolution	South Korea	1960	1960	Rhee regime
Zambian independence movement	Zambia	1961	1963	British rule
Anti-Karamanlis campaign	Greece	1963	1963	Karamanlis regime
Anti-Huong campaign	South Vietnam	1964	1965	Government of South Vietnam, Prime Minister Tran Van Huong
Anti-Tsiranana campaign	Madagascar	1972	1972	Tsiranana regime
Greek anti-military campaign	Greece	1973	1974	Military rule
Carnation Revolution	Portugal	1973	1974	Military rule
1973 Thai Uprising	Thailand	1973	1973	Military dictatorship
Pro-democracy movement	Argentina	1977	1983	Military junta
Anti-Bhutto campaign	Pakistan	1977	1977	Prime Minister Zulfikar Ali Bhutto
Bolivian anti-juntas campaign	Bolivia	1977	1982	Military juntas
Anti-Indira Campaign (Phase 3)	India	1977	1977	Prime Minister Indira Gandhi
Iranian Revolution	Iran	1977	1979	Shah Reza Pahlavi
Taiwan pro-democracy movement	Taiwan	1979	1985	Autocratic regime
Solidarity	Poland	1980	1989	Communist regime
Anti-Pinochet campaign	Chile	1983	1989	Augusto Pinochet
People Power	Philippines	1983	1986	Ferdinand Marcos
Uruguay anti-military campaign	Uruguay	1984	1985	Military rule
South African Second Defiance Campaign	South Africa	1984	1994	Apartheid
Diretas já	Brazil	1984	1985	Military rule
Anti-Duvalier campaign	Haiti	1985	1986	Jean Claude Duvalier

---

29 Based on Erica Chenoweth, *Women in Resistance Dataset*, V1 (2019), distributed by Harvard Dataverse, V3, https://doi.org/10.7910/DVN/BYFJ3Z.

Campaign	Location	Start	End	Target
Anti-Jaafar campaign	Sudan	1985	1985	Jaafar Nimeiry
South Korean anti-military movement	South Korea	1986	1987	Military government
Anti-Ershad campaign	Bangladesh	1987	1990	Military rule
Anti-PRI campaign	Mexico	1987	2000	Corrupt government
Singing Revolution	Estonia	1987	1991	Communist regime
Argentine anti-coup movement	Argentina	1987	1987	Attempted coup
Belarus anti-communist campaign	Belarus	1988	1991	Communist regime
Pro-democracy movement/Sajudis	Lithuania	1988	1991	Lithuanian regime
Timorese resistance	East Timor	1989	1999	Indonesian occupation
Mongolian anti-communist	Mongolia	1989	1990	Communist regime
Ivorian pro-democracy movement	Ivory Coast	1989	1990	Felix Houphouët Boigny regime
Benin anti-communist	Benin	1989	1990	Communist regime
Pro-democracy movement	Latvia	1989	1991	Communist regime
Velvet Revolution	Czechoslo-vakia	1989	1989	Communist regime
Public Against Violence	Slovakia	1989	1992	Czech communist government
Slovenia anti-communist	Slovenia	1989	1990	Communist regime
Pro-democracy movement	Hungary	1989	1989	Communist regime
Anti-Burnham/Hoyte campaign	Guyana	1990	1992	Burnham/Hoyte autocratic regime
Niger anti-military campaign	Niger	1990	1992	Military rule
CCCN and union pro-democracy movement	Central African Republic	1990	1993	Kolingba presidency
Kyrgyzstan Democratic Movement	Kyrgyzstan	1990	1991	Communist regime
Zambia anti-single party rule	Zambia	1990	1991	One-party rule
Mali anti-military campaign	Mali	1990	1991	Military rule
The Stir	Nepal	1990	1990	Monarchy/Panchayat regime
Students union protests	Ukraine	1990	1990	Masol Regime
Pro-democracy movement	Russia	1990	1991	Anti-coup
Slovenian independence movement	Slovenia	1990	1991	Yugoslavian rule
Albanian anti-communist	Albania	1990	1991	Communist regime

Campaign	Location	Start	End	Target
Anti-Arap Moi campaign	Kenya	1990	1991	Daniel Arap Moi
Active Voices	Madagascar	1991	1993	Didier Radsiraka
Anti-Banda campaign	Malawi	1992	1994	Banda regime
Pro-democracy movement	Thailand	1992	1992	Suchinda regime
Nigeria anti-military movement	Nigeria	1993	1999	Military rule
Anti-Milosevic movement	Serbia	1996	2000	Milosevic regime
Anti-Suharto campaign	Indonesia	1997	1998	Suharto rule
Student protests (Anti-Habibie)	Indonesia	1999	1999	President BJ Habibie
Croatian pro-democracy movement	Croatia	1999	2000	Semi-presidential system
Anti-Diouf campaign	Senegal	2000	2000	Diouf government
Anti-Fujimori campaign	Peru	2000	2000	Fujimori government
Anti-Rawlings campaign	Ghana	2000	2000	Rawlings government
Second People Power Movement	Philippines	2001	2001	Estrada regime
Anti-Chiluba campaign	Zambia	2001	2001	Chiluba regime
Nepalese anti-government	Nepal	2002	2006	Nepalese government; martial law
Pro-democracy movement	Madagascar	2002	2002	Radsiraka regime
Anti-Sanchez de Lozada Campaign	Bolivia	2003	2003	President Sanchez de Lozada
Anti-Gayoom Campaign	Maldives	2003	2008	Gayoom regime
Anti-Aristide Campaign	Haiti	2003	2004	Haitian President Jean Bertrand Aristide
Rose Revolution	Georgia	2003	2003	Shevardnadze regime
Tulip Revolution	Kyrgyzstan	2005	2005	Akayev regime
Togo anti-Gnassingbe/Coup Crisis	Togo	2005	2005	President Faure Gnassingbe Regime
Anti-Thaksin campaign	Thailand	2005	2006	Thaksin regime
Rebellion of the Forajidos	Ecuador	2005	2005	Ecuadorian President Colonel Lucio Gutierrez
Cedar Revolution	Lebanon	2005	2005	Syrian forces
Awami League Protests	Bangladesh	2006	2007	Interim government
Lebanon Political Crisis	Lebanon	2006	2008	Government of Prime Minister Fouad Siniora

Campaign	Location	Start	End	Target
Anti-Musharraf campaign (Lawyer's Movement)	Pakistan	2007	2008	Musharraf Government
Anti-Saakashvilli campaign	Georgia	2007	2013	Saakashvili Regime
Anti-Mubarak movement	Egypt	2007	2011	Government
Cutlery Revolution (Kitchenware/ Kitchen Implement Revolution)	Iceland	2008	2009	Prime Minister Geir Haarde Government
People's Alliance for Democracy Campaign	Thailand	2008	2008	People Power Party Government
Anti-Ravalomanana movement	Madagascar	2009	2009	Ravalomanana government
Second Revolution	Kyrgyzstan	2010	2010	Kyrgyz president Kurmanbek Bakiyev
Pro-Ouattara campaign	Ivory Coast	2010	2011	Gbagbo Regime
Jasmine Revolution	Tunisia	2010	2011	Ben Ali Regime
Maoist anti-government protests	Nepal	2010	2010	Madhav Kumar Nepal Government
Anti-Mutharika campaign	Malawi	2011	2012	President Mutharika Government
Anti–Ali Abdullah Saleh campaign	Yemen	2011	2012	Government (Saleh regime)
Anti-Islamist government protests	Tunisia	2013	2014	Ennahda Party
Dance with Me Campaign	Bulgaria	2013	2014	Government of Prime Minister Oresharski
Civil Movement for Democracy	Thailand	2013	2014	Yingluck government
Euromaidan	Ukraine	2013	2014	President Yanukovych
Anti-Morsi protests	Egypt	2013	2013	President Morsi

One question to consider is whether there is ever a circumstance when campaigns should seek to minimize participation? The answer is no. There is no circumstance in which low levels of participation are preferable to high levels. According to Chenoweth and Stephan:

> Over space and time, large campaigns are much more likely to succeed than small campaigns. A single unit increase of active participants makes a campaign over 10 percent more likely to achieve its ultimate outcome. Consider [Figure 16], which shows the effects of number of participants per capita on the predicted probability of campaign success. The trend is clear that as participation increases, the probability of success also increases.[30]

---

30   Chenoweth and Stephan, *Why Civil Resistance Works,* 39.

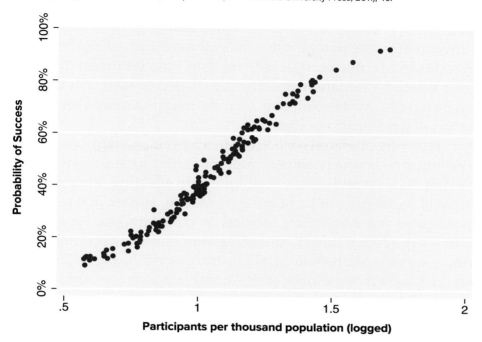

FIGURE 16: The Effect of Participation on the Probability of Campaign Success

Source: Erica Chenoweth and Maria J. Stephan, *Why Civil Resistance Works: The Strategic Logic of Nonviolent Conflict* (New York, NY: Columbia University Press, 2011), 40.

Are there threshold levels of civilian participation required for civil resistance to succeed? The answer is yes, there are threshold levels, but they are unique to each campaign and perhaps only knowable in hindsight.

In their quantitative research, Chenoweth and Stephan define "participation" in a movement as the "active and observable engagement of individuals in collective action."[31] By this measure, Chenoweth found later that 165 out of 167 nonviolent campaigns between 1945 and 2014 succeeded when they achieved participation by 3.5 percent or more of a society's population. In fact, many nonviolent campaigns succeeded with smaller levels of participation.[32]

The participation of 3.5 percent of a society's population might seem remarkably small, and in many ways it is. However, it is also

---

31 Chenoweth and Stephan, 30.

32 Erica Chenoweth, "Questions, Answers, and Some Cautionary Updates Regarding the 3.5% Rule," *Carr Discussion Paper Series,* 2020-05 (Cambridge, MA: Harvard Kennedy School, Spring 2020).

important to note that the Chenoweth–Stephan definition of "participation" looks at the highest *observable* number of people who are *visibly* engaged in civil resistance tactics in any single day (i.e., the number of people at protests or other demonstrations nationwide). Therefore, it is not necessarily representative of the full scale of movement participation, since many forms of participation in civil resistance are not easily observable to outside researchers in a post-mortem evaluation. Specifically, dispersed tactics or tactics of omission (i.e., strikes and boycotts) are much harder to measure in terms of participation rates.

For every observed participant in a movement there are also passive supporters who positively impact a civil resistance campaign by talking about it with those they know, by enabling others to more actively participate, or by offering protection, shelter, and support to persecuted pro-democracy activists or their families. An extended family of fathers, mothers, sons, daughters, aunts, uncles, and cousins may have only one person engaging in active visible participation in a conflict, but every member of the family supports the campaign and they each have a unique contact list to motivate others.

Therefore, the 3.5 percent participation threshold that Chenoweth and Stephan identify is quite likely lower than the actual number of people participating—many of whom are not necessarily visible—and certainly lower than the total number of people who support the movement's goals. Nonetheless, the 3.5 percent statistic is illustrative of just how powerful civil resistance can be. A successful civil resistance movement may require the majority of people to actively or passively support the movement or at least not stand in its way, but it does not require the majority of people to engage in high-risk mobilization at a given time in order to be effective. When thousands or millions of people decide they are going to either visibly or invisibly withdraw their support from tyrants in organized and strategic ways, tyrants do not have the capacity to continually coerce them and remain in power.

The number of dissidents who are currently active in the fight is no more important than the number of potential supporters and dissidents that are available to be recruited in the future.

The number of dissidents who are currently active in the fight is no more important than the number of potential supporters and dissidents that are available to be recruited in the future. Campaign leadership cannot be complacent with high participation rates because pro-democracy activists may lose their enthusiasm over time and become detached emotionally from the conflict. If participation rates are not maintained they will degrade, and even falling rates from exalted levels are a negative development.

One way to maintain high participation rates is to give citizens tasks that require regular engagements. Gandhi did this through his request that the Indian population use individual looms to spin their own cloth. Obedience to Gandhi's demands had three benefits: it maintained solidarity and awareness of ongoing nonviolent conflict among the masses; it created ready base of dissidents ready for more aggressive tactics; and it pressured the Lancashire textile mills by undermining the export demand for its product within India.

The current expression of Gandhi's constructive program is the creation of alternative institutions. Luke Abbs writes in his study *The Impact of Nonviolent Resistance on the Peaceful Transformation of Civil War*:

> *Alternative institutions are often formed by nonviolent campaigns to counter state institutions that may be inefficient or simply discriminatory. Alternative institutions, such as parallel education and governance systems, are self-sufficient and based on grassroots activities that can promote inclusivity.*[33]

By keeping participation rates high through the creation of alternative institutions latent double thinkers will remain encouraged to consider revealing themselves as the conflict evolves.

To mobilize people, a movement first has to analyze why people remain obedient in society in the first place. Gene Sharp cites seven core reasons why people obey oppressive systems, and others have expanded on Sharp's list. Ten core reasons are included here. Identifying which of these reasons are operative on different segments of the population, even down to the individual encounter, is an important task.

---

33 Luke Abbs, *The Impact of Nonviolent Resistance on the Peaceful Transformation of Civil War* (Washington, DC: ICNC Press, 2021), 45.

TABLE 13

1 FEAR OF PUNISHMENT

2 HABIT

3 MORAL OBLIGATION

4 SELF-INTEREST

5 PSYCHOLOGICAL IDENTIFICATION WITH THE RULER

10 CORE REASONS WHY PEOPLE OBEY OPPRESSIVE SYSTEMS

6 INDIFFERENCE + APATHY

7 LACK OF SELF-CONFIDENCE

8 IGNORANCE

9 CONFORMITY

10 COMMUNITY

■ FEAR OF PUNISHMENT

Many people obey because they fear punishment. Sanctions by the tyrant for disobedience could include loss of a job, professional reputation, privileges, status, promotion, money, property, legal rights, or community ostracism. These nonviolent sanctions can be very powerful when used selectively and strategically by a regime. The threat of further low-level sanctions by the regime can be as coercive as the actual use of harsher sanctions, including physical repression, imprisonment, torture, and death. Some people personally fear sanctions for themselves, and most fear sanctions more for the effect that the sanctions would have on their family or other people they care deeply about.

One important note about sanctions is that it is the deterrent effect which is the most powerful. States do not have the capacity to physically coerce mass obedience one person at a time, so what they do is create wholesale fear of sanctions that cause the overwhelming majority to obey at once. They do this by attacking any individual who overtly disobeys so that they can use that person as an example in order to spread fear to others.

■ HABIT

Over time, passive or active obedience to perceived authority can become habitual. From years of conditioning, people may stop questioning why they do what they do. When an accepted authority figure (e.g., a boss, religious leader, community elder, teacher, doctor, the head of their household) tells them to do something, they follow the orders without thinking.

■ MORAL OBLIGATION

Some people obey oppressive laws or practices because they feel that it is their moral obligation to do so. They may think that their obedience is for the common good of society or for the continuation of a cultural or religious tradition that is more important than their individual preferences for freedom.

■ SELF-INTEREST

Self-interest is a powerful motivator. Money, employment, social status, family security, university admission, access to good healthcare, and other material benefits or privileges can all induce obedience. Some states try to employ many people directly so that they can connect those people's self-interest to the viability of the state. Members of the business community are also often tied to the status quo by self-interest.

■ PSYCHOLOGICAL IDENTIFICATION WITH THE RULER

Some rulers try to present themselves as fathers of a tribe, ethnic group, or nation. People feel almost a familial connection with these rulers, trust them beyond reason, are emotionally bonded to them, and feel that what is good for the rulers is what is good for their ethnic group or nation. Sometimes these rulers have led a nation through a particular historic moment (such as a struggle against a colonial power) that is then mythologized and becomes a basis for their claim to enduring legitimacy. In other cases, the ruler claims some sort of religious or ideological authority that makes them seem inherently correct and beyond normal criticism.

■ INDIFFERENCE AND APATHY

People may submit to oppressive rule because they claim they do not care about politics and are indifferent or apathetic to the suffering that the tyrant creates. They may say that suffering is "the way it is and the way it has always been" and therefore not worth getting worked up about. However, claims of indifference and apathy may disguise deeper feelings of helplessness. Many people actually would do something about their oppression if they felt they could have an impact or knew more precisely what they could do.

■ LACK OF SELF-CONFIDENCE

Tyrants intentionally project an image of invincibility to try to destroy people's confidence in their ability to successfully challenge the system or believe that there is any alternative to the tyrant's rule. Tyrants repress opposition groups to the point that they claim there are no other groups or leaders qualified to rule. If there are any cases where people have tried to challenge the tyrant and failed, the tyrant will create large amounts of propaganda about those cases to reinforce feelings of hopelessness among the general population.

■ IGNORANCE

Information is power, and tyrants do their best to keep their people ignorant of the regime's corruption, incompetence, cronyism, and abuses (except for those abuses that they deliberately publicize to create fear among the population). Tyrants blame others for any hardship that the country endures. When a civil resistance movement challenges the tyrant on issues like corruption, human rights abuses, or lack of government accountability, the tyrant claims that thousands or millions of civil resisters are themselves part of an external conspiracy and a threat to the nation. One would think that tyrants can never convincingly explain how thousands or millions of people personally volunteering their time to participate in a pro-democracy campaign, incurring risk, making sacrifices, and working together for a common purpose is explicable through the act of some foreign power. Yet, out of ignorance, some people will believe this is a possibility and continue to obey the tyrant for this reason.

■ CONFORMITY

People feel safe in numbers. When a lot of people are obeying, an individual is more likely to join them than stand separately. There exists a real fear of nonconformity, and it is hard and risky to be the first individuals who stop conforming, ask difficult questions, and risk losing the benefits of anonymity and blending in.

■ COMMUNITY

A sense of community can be a very strong motivator for consent and obedience. If a community provides people with a sense of identity, meaning, belonging, and validation, people will take strong actions to remain part of that community, even if they personally disagree with how the community chooses to act during the nonviolent conflict. Communities can also engage in peer pressure or set social expectations in a way that causes people to doubt or ignore their own judgment, so they are not thinking critically anymore about what they are doing in the name of preserving their community.

The leaders of a nonviolent conflict need to inventory their universe of supporters with a high level of granularity. They need to understand the precise reasons for individual passivity and resignation and find ways to motivate specific actions helpful to the campaign. The good news is that when those who are initially reluctant decide to complete any task (large or small) as part of the civil resistance, their appetite often will grow to do more. The same is true for former dissidents: one simple act of opposition can remind them of their power and reignite their passion to be part of a winning civil resistance campaign.

CHECKLIST QUESTION #6 | Is the tyrant's belief in the efficacy of violent repression likely to diminish?

Just as athletic contests are unpredictable due to large swings in the relative levels of confidence of the players, a tyrant's belief in the efficacy of violent repression and his actual capacity to unleash it also depend on his confidence. But how does one gauge whether a tyrant's confidence is increasing or decreasing? It is difficult enough to measure the current status of a tyrant's beliefs but seemingly impossible to predict how these beliefs will evolve over time.

Ivan Marovic, one of the leaders of the Otpor student movement that precipitated the fall of Slobodan Milosevic in Serbia, offers a relevant insight. He suggests that recognizing the diminishing levels of violence "happens from the outside in." The tyrant may be the last to know his repression is backfiring, as there are several leading indicators that are more apparent to pro-democracy activists. Dissidents will experience more freedom of movement encouraging them to engage in more high profile disruptions. Latent double thinkers may be quicker to reveal themselves because the fear of reprisal is much lower. And potential defectors—particularly from the military and police—will realize that by merely threatening to refuse to be the agents of violence, they can severely restrict the tyrant's options to use force.

Tyrants can find more than a few good reasons to use violence against a people power movement. Indeed, from 1900 to 2006, 88 percent of all insurrections (violent and nonviolent) were met with violence. Furthermore, the success rate of a civil resistance campaign drops by approximately a third when it encounters violent repression.

Violence can curtail a movement's leadership, restrict freedom of movement and speech, and seize needed assets to deprive families of shelter, food, and medicine. Furthermore, violence can create divisions by repressing one faction while offering concessions to another. Finally, violence can tempt members of a civil resistance who are the most frustrated and fearful to break with their commitment to nonviolent discipline. The cumulative impact of frequent repression can reinforce a sense of fear and powerlessness in a population, and thwart independent communications and travel. These possibilities are the reasons why tyrants resort to violence when in a strong position.

Dictators may find the argument for violence even more compelling when their power is in decline. When the use of repression is believed to be the decisive factor for whether a dictatorship will endure, then the correct strategy for the dictator should be to increase the brutality until a nonviolent conflict is defeated. The logical consequence of this argument is that a tyrant's willingness to use violence should remain high and never waiver. However, this perspective is based on two faulty assumptions:

- That a tyrant's capacity for repression does not change during the course of a nonviolent conflict; and

- That the impact of a tyrant's repression does not change through the course of the conflict.

During a nonviolent conflict, these variables can fluctuate dramatically, making it difficult for a tyrant to assess the value of each increment of repression. Strategic decisions made by dissidents—particularly with respect to maintaining high levels of civilian participation and strict nonviolent discipline—can intensify these fluctuations, leaving the tyrant unsure of whether his repression can keep him in power.

The default position for a tyrant is to depend on increasingly brutal repression as the regime's hold on power weakens. Resorting to more brutal tactics is not necessarily a sign of strength but can be a leading indicator that the tyrant's defeat is imminent. It is at this moment of greatest weakness that dictators' orders to police and military are most likely to be disobeyed.

Perception is key, but reality plays a part since relying on violence for political control is never cost-free to the tyrant. The most tangible costs of repression to a regime are the allocation of human resources, material resources, and money. Repression requires people, equipment (e.g., vehicles, riot gear, weapons, monitoring technology, prisons, courts), and money to compensate enforcers. It is expensive to pay police day-after-day to deploy themselves in the streets to investigate pro-democracy activists and bring them to prison. It can become even more costly to figure out what to do with mass incarceration. Regimes can accept these costs so long as they create enough fear to keep the rest of society hesitant and obedient. However, in the face of sustained mass resistance, the financial burden of ongoing repression can rapidly become unsustainable.

Public demonstrations—perhaps the most visible nonviolent tactic—will become unmanageable for a regime when they are dispersed geographically. When protest demonstrations are happening in cities and towns all over the country, regime security forces will get stretched thin. They cannot effectively concentrate in any one area and the regime's ability to control public demonstrations will become severely compromised.

Now consider how the pressure increases if a campaign simultaneously engages in decentralized actions such as consumer boycotts. In such a scenario, how can police possibly figure out who is participating in the boycott? Who do they arrest? If there are millions engaged in work stoppages all over the country, how can the security forces find them and arrest them all?

In addition to the human, material, and financial costs of trying to subdue a campaign of civil resistance, a regime's use of violent repression entails the risk of lost legitimacy. The regime is revealed to be violating the values that it claims to cherish and betraying the trust of people that it claims to represent. When nonviolent dissidents advocate for freedom and widely shared political beliefs, violent repression used against them will severely damage a regime's hold on the public imagination.

People may begin to see the tyrant not as a strong patriotic protector of the nation and its citizens, but rather as someone who is willing to sacrifice the public good to protect his own private interests. Tyrants put a great deal of effort into making their personal image synonymous with the image of the country and the flag. They do this in order to create the impression that any criticism of the tyrant is anti-patriotic or treasonous. But when it is revealed that a tyrant will use any state resources to protect himself from popular, organized, nonviolent dissent, the tyrant is no longer able to claim patriotism as a basis for his legitimacy. He is seen as an ordinary man, a criminal, a traitor of the people, or an occupier, who, together with his small group of cronies, are preying on a society and exploiting public resources for selfish reasons.

As the authoritarian's legitimacy begins to erode, pro-democracy activists can sense the growing commitment of their base. Passive supporters become more active and more willing to assume risk. Neutral or uninvolved groups become offended by the indefensible violence of the tyrant. The tyrant's nonstop repression shatters the illusions that some people may hold about his virtue, the purpose of his regime, and even the ongoing viability of the status quo. The tyrant becomes aware of the heightened risks of how continued violence may cause higher numbers of loyalty shifts and defections among his supporters and thus finds himself in an existential dilemma.

If there are millions engaged in work stoppages, how can the security forces find them and arrest them all?

Adding to the dilemma, increased violent repression will lead to heightened attention and scrutiny by international actors. These include multilateral institutions, international nongovernmental organizations, journalists, and diaspora communities. Even states that are allied with the tyrant may shift their loyalties or temper their support as a tyrant's brutality is exposed. In general, increased international attention brought by a tyrant's repression will lead to shifting calculations among external actors about how they should behave towards the conflict. These developments can be negative for the tyrant if one of his country's allies fully turns against him.

The most devastating risk for a tyrant is the one in which he commands the use of violence against citizens and his lieutenants refuse to comply. This refusal puts the tyrant in mortal jeopardy unless the dissidents release the pressure by encouraging a violent flank or by breaking with nonviolent discipline. Faced with the risk of violence against them, to defend themselves his lieutenants will obey the tyrant's demand for violence.

A skillful leader of a civil resistance campaign must keep the prospect of noncompliance to the tyrants' orders uppermost in the tyrant's mind. One way to do this is to diversify by sequencing tactics of commission and concentration with tactics of omission and dispersion in order to stay in the fight and weather repression. As long as that capacity exists and is executed with increasing skill, the tyrant will eventually lose confidence that repression can be the ultimate weapon to prevent a loss of power. It is the existence of these strategic skills that explain why a civil resistance campaign is twice as likely to succeed as is a violent insurrection.

However, some note that what has been true in the past may not necessarily be true in the future. For example, one could argue that today's newest technologies have permanently conferred advantages for tyrants in their battles with dissidents. In a recent article in *Foreign Affairs* titled "Digital Dictators: How Technology Strengthens Autocracy" written by Andrea Kendall-Taylor, Erica Frantz, and Joseph Wright, the authors observe:

> *The advancement of AI-powered surveillance is the most significant evolution in digital authoritarianism. High-resolution cameras, facial recognition, spying malware, automated text analysis, and big-data processing have opened up a wide range of new methods of citizen control.* [34]

The authors also believe that technology strengthens the link between repression and obedience that the dissident hopes to dissolve. In the same article they note:

> *Dictatorships harness technology not only to suppress protests but also to stiffen older methods of control. Our analysis... suggests that dictatorships that increase their use of digital repression also tend to increase their use of violent forms of repression "in real life," particularly torture and the killing of opponents. This indicates that authoritarian leaders don't replace traditional repression with digital repression. Instead, by making it easier for authoritarian regimes to identify their opposition, digital repression allows them to more effectively determine who should get a knock on the door or be thrown in a cell. This closer targeting of opponents reduces the need to resort to indiscriminate repression, which can trigger a popular backlash and elite defections.* [35]

---

34 Andrea Kendall-Taylor, Erica Frantz, and Joseph Wright, "The Digital Dictators: How Technology Strengthens Autocracy," in *Foreign Affairs* (March/April 2020), https://www.foreignaffairs.com/articles/china/2020-02-06/digital-dictators

35 Kendall-Taylor, Frantz, and Wright, "Digital Dictators."

Is this the end of discussion? Will current advances in technology continue to advantage tyrants until they are the winner in every nonviolent conflict going forward? This is very unlikely. Twenty-six years ago, I observed:

> *A final factor that is transforming the environment of conflict is technology, and especially communications technology. Since organized social conflict requires improved access to cheap, efficient, and discreet communications should make strategic nonviolent conflict both easier to perform and more relevant. Indeed, new technologies from personal computing to fax machines, beepers, and cellular telephones have already created a whole new range of opportunities for practitioners of nonviolent struggle. Despite many impressive examples of strategists exploiting these new opportunities, we must note that technological advances confer no permanent advantage on those who are democratic and nonviolent. The same tools can be used for domination and repression. They do not relieve nonviolent strategists of their fundamental strategic obligation: to outperform their adversaries.* [36]

We should therefore not assume that new technological developments will convey a permanent benefit to the tyrant over the dissident, as the situation can rapidly reverse. For example, today the food industry uses very small radio frequency tags to track totes that hold products for home delivery. Imagine taking that tag, improving the range of transmission, and putting it on a postage stamp-sized card with adhesive on the other side. Send millions of tags into Iran, China, and Russia or other authoritarian country. Dissidents will now have a new form of signage to put on outdoor walls to express subversive messages or to communicate how and where to execute a specific nonviolent tactic. Another example of technological opportunity could be a lapel pin that gives off a signal to make an individual's face undetectable for state high-resolution scanners placed on the streets. Or a small flashlight device that burns a surveillance camera lens, rendering it useless. Furthermore, is there any reason that the newest and most damaging forms of malware will be available only for the use of tyrants?

---

36 Peter Ackerman and Christopher Kruegler, *Strategic Nonviolent Conflict: The Dynamics of People Power in the Twentieth Century* (Westport, CT: Praeger Publishers, 1994), xxiii.

Kendall-Taylor, Frantz, and Wright, the authors of "Digital Dictators," point out the most pernicious (and clever) uses of artificial intelligence (AI) in China:

> No regime has exploited the repressive potential of AI quite as thoroughly as the one in China. The Chinese Communist Party collects an incredible amount of data on individuals and businesses: tax returns, bank statements, purchasing histories, and criminal and medical records. The regime then uses AI to analyze this information and compiles "social credit scores," which it seeks to use to set the parameters of acceptable behavior and improve citizen control. Individuals or companies deemed "untrustworthy" can find themselves excluded from state-sponsored benefits, such as deposit-free apartment rentals, or banned from air and rail travel. Although the CCP is still honing this system, advances in big-data analysis and decision-making technologies will only improve the regime's capacity for predictive control, what the government calls "social management."[37]

If AI can be used for social control, then applications could be developed as a means for dissidents to identify potential regime defectors. For example, there should be a way to allow people to engage in anonymous referenda to signal their evolving loyalties and preferences. Such a capability would provide an opportunity to reveal a society's authentic preferences. This could prove that an authoritarian's support is much weaker than generally assumed, potentially paving the way for greater civil disobedience.

The billions of dollars spent by China today may lead to overreliance on technological products that will invariably degrade. In the not-so-distant future, tyrants relying primarily on technology to stay in power may instead find they have created a modern example of the Maginot Line that is more imagined than real.

CHECKLIST QUESTION #7 | Are potential defections among the tyrant's key supporters likely to increase?

Unless the tyrant and his closest allies have a crisis of faith and unilaterally renounce their power, nonviolent conflicts cannot succeed without defections, especially among security forces.

---

37 Kendall-Taylor, Frantz, and Wright, "Digital Dictators."

Defections have the greatest benefit if they occur among supporters on which the tyrant most depends to exert his control over the population. To the extent that a defection surprises the tyrant, it will create hesitation in his use of force because he will become uncertain as to which of his allies will disappoint him next.

A common misconception about tyrannical governments is that they are monolithic and that their supporters are forever united. But tyrannies depend on the support of many different individuals and groups—including business owners, laborers, bankers, bureaucrats, police officers, members of the military, judges, leaders of religious organizations, and workers in transportation, communications, and infrastructure, among others. Each have their own interests, goals, culture, history, networks, and rivals. A tyrannical regime can function efficiently only to the extent that these diverse individuals and groups control their disagreements amongst one another, moderate their divergent interests, and take cooperative action to support the regime. To the extent there is opposition, the tyrant must keep it muted and isolated.

Most political realists think the capacities of these constituencies are fixed conditions over which a nonviolent movement has very little influence. The strength of a security force, for example, is calculated based on budget, equipment, personnel, training, and experience. It is assumed by realists that a civil resistance campaign confronts a tyrant who has consistent repressive capacity at his command. But history shows that civil resistance movements are able to erode the capabilities and cohesion of a tyrant's security services over time. Dissidents have accomplished this by aggravating the differences between individuals and units within the security services, by increasing uncertainty that the status quo can be maintained and by catalyzing defections.

Security forces are not the only group that defects from a tyrant during the course of a conflict, but they are the group that has received the most research interest. In a comparative study of Serbia (2000) and Ukraine (2004), Anika Binnendijk and Ivan Marovic made the following conclusion about the significance of military defection in nonviolent conflict:

> Strategic attention to state security forces may serve three major functions of force on the battlefield of a nonviolent struggle: defence, deterrence, and compellent. Defensively, it may mute the impact of

a regime's violent weapons again the movement and its allies (Ackerman and Kruegler, 1994). As the costs of repression mount and capacity to suppress opposition diminishes, the regime leadership may be deterred from attempting to wield coercive force at all (Dahl, 1971). Finally, by weakening one of the regime's core centers of gravity, a movement may compel it into new election standards, or even removal from office.[38]

Chenoweth and Stephan have identified cases of "large-scale, systematic breakdowns [by security forces] in the execution of a regime's orders"[39] during civil resistance movements, and they have found that the presence of such defections increases the movement's probability of success by 58 percent.

Below are eleven important examples where security force defections have had a decisive influence on the outcome of a nonviolent conflict.

TABLE 14: Nonviolent Campaigns with Significant Security Force Defections	
Campaign	**Year**
Nonviolent revolution against Shah Mohammad Reza Pahlavi in Iran	**1978–79**
Campaign against a military dictatorship in Chile	**1985–1988**
People Power in the Philippines	**1983–1986**
Nonviolent resistance against August Putsch in the Soviet Union	**1990**
Bulldozer Revolution in Serbia	**2000**
Orange Revolution in Ukraine	**2004**
Jasmine Revolution in Tunisia	**2011**
Burkinabé uprising against President Blaise Compaoré in Burkina Faso	**2014**
Velvet Revolution in Armenia	**2018**
Popular uprising against President Evo Morales in Bolivia	**2018–2019**
Algeria's Revolution of Smiles	**2019–2020**

38 Anika Binnendijk and Ivan Marovic, "Power and Persuasion: Nonviolent Strategies to Influence State Security Forces in Serbia (2000) and Ukraine (2004)," in *Communist and Post-Communist Studies* 39, no. 3 (September 2006): 411–429.

39 Chenoweth and Stephan, *Why Civil Resistance Works,* 48.

The research by Chenoweth and Stephan does not focus on routine individual defections from security forces, nor does it link success rates of campaigns to defections from leaders of the judiciary, business community, political parties, state-run media, bureaucracies, religious institutions, or revered cultural figures. However, as a standard rule we can conclude all defections from an authoritarian regime are helpful for pro-democracy activists.

Achieving defections by the tyrant's closest allies is significantly harder than mobilizing average citizens to participate in nonviolent conflict. A dissident who has second thoughts is able to retreat after participating in a single nonviolent tactical encounter against the tyrant. However, once a prominent latent double thinker emerges as a revealed double thinker, there is no going back. When key loyalties shift, they shift for the duration of the conflict.

As the numbers of campaign participants grow, the numbers of potential defectors will grow as well. Conversely as campaign participation shrinks, latent double thinkers will choose to remain hidden until they perceive a reversal of momentum in favor of the dissidents. This is why defections are more likely to occur in the middle to later stages of nonviolent conflicts.

What types of arguments encourage citizens to defect from a tyrannical regime? There is no formula or one size fits all approach to potential defectors who are all taking unique risks. Gene Sharp conceived and identified four mechanisms of change in the course of an entire conflict that are triggered by successful civil resistance movements.[40] Each of these mechanisms describe a way that civil resistance campaigns can alter an individual's attitudes and behavior, and they aptly describe four ways a defector is induced to publicly renounce tyranny:

- Conversion;
- Accommodation;
- Coercion; and
- Disintegration.

---

40 Gene Sharp, *The Politics of Nonviolent Action, Part Three: The Dynamics of Nonviolent Action* (Boston, MA: Porter Sargent Publishers, 1973).

■ CONVERSION

In conversion, a movement is able to persuade a person or group that its cause is worth supporting on its merits alone. Potential defectors begin as loyalists to the regime. For a significant period of their lives they will have worked hard to make the regime successful. To convince a latent double thinker to renounce that mission, dissidents must initially create cognitive dissonance. This requires multiple contacts. Potential defectors need to be actively cultivated by leaders of civil resistance efforts if they are to be converted. Pro-democracy activists must continually expand the list of potential converts by regularly dialoguing with those who may have a proclivity to defect.

Through nonviolent tactics that disrupt the status quo, alongside culturally empathetic communication a civil resistance campaign can create cognitive dissonance in supposedly loyal people. Potential defectors gradually become more sensitive to the lies upon which the regime is based and begin to realize the regime is exploiting people—including them—for its own gain. Key individuals may begin to see the nonviolent movement as the true representative of popular aspirations. During the conversion process, hope and confidence begin to replace despair and disorientation. Double thinkers begin to reveal themselves in greater numbers as the risks of conversion diminish. Confidence increases in the campaign's prospects of success as the tyrant's vulnerabilities become more apparent.

■ ACCOMMODATION

Accommodation means that a person or group makes a cost–benefit analysis and decides that their self-interest lies in shifting their loyalties away from the regime. Frequently this happens among businessmen and other economic elites who, through the course of a civil resistance movement, realize they may lose increasing amounts of money by continuing to passively or actively ally themselves with the regime. Because business owners are primarily concerned with maintaining the value of their economic interests, supporting the authoritarian is much more a matter of expedience than principle. If the tyrant becomes more oppressive, they may come to see that accommodating a civil resistance campaign's demands via defection is the most effective way to protect their financial position. When a campaign of civil resistance jeopardizes the financial interests of both owners and workers alike, the question of whether continued complicity in the tyrant's immoral rule becomes even more urgent.

■ COERCION

Coercion takes place when those who actively oppose a civil resistance campaign defect from a tyrant out of fear of the consequences of continued support for the tyrant. This can happen when former allies become convinced that a tyrant's rule is going to come to an end, so their ongoing loyalty to the tyrant is no longer the safe option. Instead, they start to question how they can best position themselves for what seems like an inevitable victory for the civil resistance followed by a transition period. There are many instances of loyal backers of tyrants ultimately defecting when they began to feel that the tyrant was finished, which in turn weakens the tyrant further and sets up a self-fulfilling prophecy.

■ DISINTEGRATION

With disintegration, a regime rapidly and uncontrollably crumbles. In this case, there is no regime left to be loyal to. This is often a dangerous situation for dissidents unless they can quickly fill the power vacuum with a popular and achievable transition plan. Without clarity as to what form of governance should come next, former regime supporters and the military may organize themselves to constitute a new regime, attempt a coup and try to "restore stability" through force of arms. To protect against this possibility, pro-democracy activists can increase their dialogue with those they targeted for defection. They can also develop a transition process and plan in the earlier phases of their campaign, and this can serve as a template when it is needed.

These mechanisms of change over time describe how disloyalties can fester and burst open to undermine dictatorships. This is why not all defections begin with acts that are necessarily public and overt. Defections may take the form of simply carrying out orders slowly or inefficiently. They may include anonymous acts of sabotage or deliberate misfiling of important documents. They may include starting underground negotiations with civil resistance movement leaders and passing information and resources along to them. Most of these subtle and low-level acts of defection are incredibly difficult for a regime to discover or confront. While open insubordination is easy to identify and punish, deliberate incompetence and secret disobedience is much more difficult to counter.

Defections from one group or subgroup can accelerate defections from others. Economist and political scientist Timur Kuran explains that those who are dissatisfied (for any reason) with a regime face a simple choice between publicly expressing their true preference (which is anti-regime) or falsifying their true preference by expressing support for the regime.[41] People who choose to hide their true preferences face an inner psychological cost for doing so. They will still continue to obey the regime until the external risks for doing so exceed the benefits of expressing their true preferences.

Different people have different thresholds of risk tolerance when it comes to exposing their true preference. For some, the inner psychological toll of continued preference falsification is so high that they decide early in the nonviolent conflict they must express their true feelings against the regime. As they do this, it begins to shift the calculations of other onlookers who are also engaged in preference falsification. As the onlookers begin to see more and more people defecting, they too decide to defect. As more people defect, the benefits of defection are seen to exceed the benefits of ongoing obedience to the regime.

While I was the Chairman of Freedom House between the years of 2005 and 2009, one of my co-chairs was Mark Palmer. Mark was an American icon for advancing democracy. His famous book, *Breaking the Real Axis of Evil: How to Oust the World's Last Dictators by 2025,* was motivated by the same values as this volume. Mark was the United States Ambassador to Hungary during the momentous years of 1986–1990. He told me that during this volatile period he was approached by the Hungarian minister of propaganda. Seeing his position under threat, he asked Mark what job he could possibly do in a post-Communist Hungary. Mark had a quick response: "Why, of course, you should start a communications company." Mark told me that this was precisely what the former minister of propaganda ended up doing. Think of the comfort Mark's words must have been to him. His fear of the abyss, of some ill-defined but dangerous "transitional justice," was dissolved and replaced by hope and optimism about his future. This allowed the minister of propaganda to

---

41   Timur Kuran, *Private Truths, Public Lies* (Cambridge, MA: Harvard University Press, 1995).

cease clinging to his instrumental role in propping up the increasingly illegitimate Communist leadership.

Kuran labels the point at which a person chooses to express their true preference against a regime as a "revolutionary threshold." He points out that although different people have different revolutionary thresholds, cascading defections can occur as those with lower thresholds for defection begin to trigger defections from those with higher thresholds. Some people may be willing to defect if they believe one percent of the population is already doing so. As those people with a "one percent" revolutionary threshold join the movement, their participation bumps up the total movement participation to two percent of the population. This in turn triggers people with a "two percent" revolutionary threshold, whose participation then bumps total movement participation to three percent of the population, which then triggers the next round of defections, and so forth.

Answers to certain checklist questions are critical to catalyzing pathways to defection. These include civilian participation (Checklist Question 5), nonviolent discipline (Checklist Question 2) and strategic planning (Checklist Question 3).

Chenoweth and Stephan show that high levels of civilian participation significantly increase the probability of security force defections. They find that "for nonviolent campaigns, the probability of security-force defections steadily increases as membership in the resistance campaign grows" and that "the largest nonviolent campaigns have about a 60 percent chance of producing security-force defections, an increase of over 50 percent from the smallest nonviolent campaigns."[42] The more people who participate in a civil resistance, the more ties they will have to the regime's supporters, whether based on kinship or personal or professional affiliations. All of these points of contact can be used to exert influence and trigger defections.

Another aspect of the Checklist that helps lead to defections is maintaining nonviolent discipline. A tyrant's supporter will never signal an intention to defect if they feel threatened physically. Furthermore, because nonviolent discipline correlates with high levels of public participation in movements, the maintenance of nonviolent discipline can also indirectly contribute to inducing defections.

---

42   Chenoweth and Stephan, *Why Civil Resistance Works*, 48.

In contrast, while security force defections can and do happen in the midst of violent insurgencies, they happen less frequently. This makes sense for several reasons. Violent insurgencies can actually increase cohesion between a regime and its supporters, who feel united by a common threat. Security forces are unlikely to believe that they will be safe from retribution if they shift loyalties to a violent insurgency.

Every strategy for winning civil resistance campaigns will need to consider detailed planning to maximize defections through conscious sequencing of tactics. Every potential group and its individual members should be targeted, and multiple contacts made. It is not a realistic expectation that a single engagement will transform latent double thinkers into active dissidents. There are occasions where individuals are ripe for this transformation but need additional encouragement. Controversial ideas need time to ripen in individual consciousness. Usually this goes through four phases:

- Defection? A terrible idea for me filled with danger.
- Defection? I've heard this is a possibility from others.
- Defection? I knew this made sense all along.
- Defection? This was my idea from the start.

To understand how to drive defections, a critical first step is fact finding and assessment. The more familiarity with members of the particular group that pro-democracy activists want to influence, the better equipped those activists will be to develop effective customized tactics and communications. Detailed knowledge of individual tendencies is critical.

To be thorough, a plan for interaction needs to be developed for every group, subgroup, and individual who prop up the tyranny. Then, priorities must be established for who should be primary targets for defection. Flexibility in targeting is also key since the success or failure of any tactic may determine which latent double thinkers to speak with next.

Probably nothing in a nonviolent campaign correlates more neatly with success than expanding dialogue with a cohort of latent double thinkers. As long as the movement is experiencing positive momentum, they can continue to push an unstoppable wave of defections from which a tyrant is unlikely to recover.

CHECKLIST QUESTION #8 | Is a post-conflict political order likely to emerge consistent with democratic values?

A successful campaign against a tyrannical regime is most likely to lead to democracy if it is driven by civil resistance. Dissidents can be highly confident of this assertion as there are multiple sources of supporting data. One of these is an important study by scholar Jonathan Pinckney, who examined 331 transitions among non-democratic regimes, which included 78 that were induced by civil resistance.[43]

Commenting on the array of countries in which civil resistance drove a political transition, Pinckney finds that "the countries are highly diverse. This is not simply a Latin American story, or an African story, or a European story, but the story of a global phenomenon that has had deeply transformational effects."[44]

After conducting statistical analysis, his key conclusion is that:

The independent effects of nonviolent resistance on democracy are substantial ... if nonviolent resistance initiates a transition, it more than doubles the likelihood that the country will end its transition

FIGURE 17: Countries with at Least One Civil Resistance-Induced Transition (1945–2015)

Source: Jonathan Pinckney, *When Civil Resistance Succeeds: Building Democracy After Popular Nonviolent Uprisings* (Washington, DC: ICNC Press, 2018), 27.

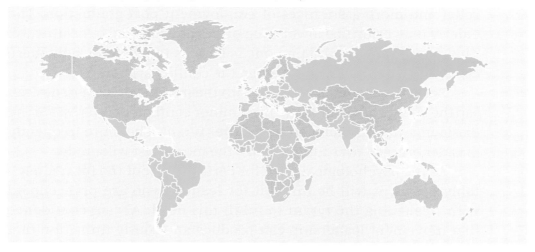

■ Countries with at least one civil resistance-induced transition from **1945 to 2015**

---

43 Jonathan Pinckney, *When Civil Resistance Succeeds: Building Democracy After Popular Nonviolent Uprisings* (Washington, DC: ICNC Press, 2018).

44 Pinckney, *When Civil Resistance Succeeds*, 27.

with at least some basic minimum level of democracy.... Without civil resistance, the probability of crossing the democratic threshold at the end of a transition is roughly 30%. With civil resistance, this probability jumps to around 70%.[45]

Pinckney's finding of a 70 percent probability of a democratic outcome after a successful civil resistance campaign validates the impact of a nonviolent uprising.

However, it also should cause us to reflect on the fact that 30 percent of successful civil resistance campaigns do not achieve democratic transitions. This shows that even as a civil resistance campaign is winning, there remain risks that it will not achieve a democratic order. How can pro-democracy activists address these risks?

Unifying during early stages of a nonviolent conflict around common aspirations to unseat a tyrant is one challenge, but achieving detailed agreement about how institutions of government will distribute benefits once the tyrant is gone is another. For example, farmers may want cheaper mortgage rates and the continuation of subsidies to sell their goods for adequate prices. People in urban areas may be concerned with clean water and improved public safety. Public sector unions may demand earlier retirement dates and more lucrative pensions. Working parents may want better job prospects and minimum wages. Students may demand scholarship relief and more assurances of employment post-graduation. The elderly may prioritize lower drug prices and affordable healthcare. This list may grow while no one is sure as to whom or how these concerns will be prioritized when the conflict is over.

Being preoccupied early on with the minutia of local issues can sap the energy of a campaign. Even minor conflicts of interest among dissidents can be exploited by a clever tyrant. The more frequently dissidents argue over future spoils, the more trust will erode.

As the psychological need for certainty about the future inevitably grows, it will be difficult for leaders who are preoccupied with weakening the tyrant to fulfill this need. Absent confidence that movement leadership can produce an orderly transition that improves people's lives, at some point people may put their desire for predictable (even if meager) material well-being offered by the tyrant ahead of an ill-defined transition to "democracy."

---

45 Pinckney, *When Civil Resistance Succeeds*, 38.

*Gandhi arrives in Britain for negotiations after the successful
Salt March for Indian Independence, 1931.*

Further, the more that tensions emerge among pro-democracy activists, the less likely latent double thinkers will reveal themselves. On the other hand, some generally accepted ideas about what the post-conflict order will bring may give key supporters of the existing regime the confidence to defect.

In some circumstances, the organizers of a civil resistance campaign may need to defer to the political leaders who will be important to inspire the population to accept a post-tyrannical order. During the anti-apartheid struggle in South Africa, there were 300 civic groups in the 1980s who acted as surrogates for the African National Congress (ANC) leaders who were in jail. In fact, those still imprisoned were the beneficiaries of the civil resistance campaign even though they did not necessarily embrace the strategy that set them free. Nelson Mandela never renounced the use of violence to end apartheid. Despite his revered status, the anti-apartheid movement leadership became committed to engaging in a civil resistance campaign after the frustration of the unsuccessful reliance on guerilla violence in the 1970s. One of the best examples of the new 1980s face of nonviolent conflict was the Port Elizabeth consumer boycott led by Mkhuseli Jack, as documented in the film *A Force More Powerful*.[46]

---

46 The documentary is available in several languages at the following webpage:
    https://www.nonviolent-conflict.org/force-powerful-english/.

While Mandela's openness to using violence against apartheid was not strategically sound, it should not belittle his critical role and genius once he was out of jail. He was so successful in his politics that he put in motion a nonviolent transfer of power, culminating in free elections that made him the first post-apartheid president of South Africa.

One of Iran's most prominent dissidents claims that millions of Iranian citizens who oppose the regime are in agreement about democracy, secularism, the Universal Declaration of Human Rights, equal civil rights for all Iranians (regardless of religion, sex, or ethnicity), and commitment to a civil resistance campaign to bring down the mullahs while avoiding armed struggle. He notes that there are also areas of disagreement or areas where people "agree to agree" in the future. These include whether the symbol of the country will be a king or an elected president in the future democracy of Iran, and the details of running the country by the people including how power will be distributed in different regions.

Well-known dissident and author Bill Moyer observes that movements must win at least two victories: First, they must defeat what they stand against, and second, they must win what they stand for. There is no one size fits all playbook to link the two victories.

To every extent possible, nonviolent tactics should be designed to foster cooperative behavior among those with potential competitive interests in a post-tyrannical society. Trust comes after people with diverse priorities stand shoulder to shoulder when taking risks during the nonviolent conflict.

In 2005, I co-authored the study, *How Freedom is Won: From Civic Struggle to Durable Democracy*. It reviewed 67 transitions over the prior 33 years and concluded the following:

> *Internally, broad-based civic coalitions are environments for compromise, common ground, and self-discipline. As separate groupings learn to work with others who hold different political beliefs, they create a basis for the tolerant give-and-take that is a crucial component of democracy. At the same time, mass-based civic movements become an important school for the preparation of future civic leaders, politicians, opinion makers, and government leaders in the post-transition period. They become a mechanism for the emergence*

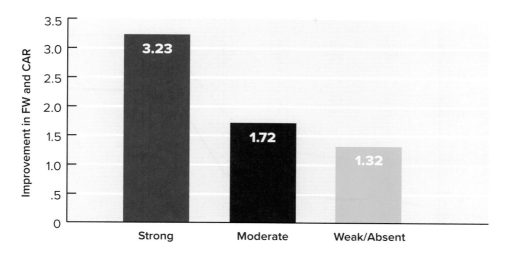

FIGURE 18: The Stronger a Nonviolent Civic Coalition, the Larger the Gains for Freedom

Source: Karatnycky and Ackerman, *How Freedom Is Won*, 18.

FIW = "Freedom in the World" CAR = "Combined Average Rating" (average of FIW Political Rights and Civil Liberties scores. The scores are based on a 1-7 scale: 1 represents the highest level of freedom and 7 the lowest.)

of a new leadership cohort, often creating a talent pool that can sustain the transition toward freedom.

In short, broad-based democracy coalitions can imbue leaders and activists with the principles and experience that make for successful democratic governance.[47]

Figure 18 sorts the 67 transitions into three categories based on the strength of civic coalitions: strong, moderate, and weak/absent. The study analyzed the gains in political rights and civil liberties using Freedom House's Combined Average Rating (CAR) scores in the Freedom in the World index.[48]

Combined average ratings for each country, applied consistently year to year, can be uniquely aggregated to illustrate worldwide trends

---

47 Adrian Karatnycky and Peter Ackerman, *How Freedom Is Won: From Civic Struggle to Durable Democracy* (Washington, DC: Freedom House, 2005), 12.

48 Every year since 1972, Freedom House ranks each country from 1 (most free) to 7 (least free). They assign the ratings by two matrices—political rights and civil liberties—as defined by the Universal Declaration of Human Rights. The average of these two numbers is the combined average rating (CAR). For example, since inception, North Korea has never improved on its double seven ranking, which is a CAR of 7.

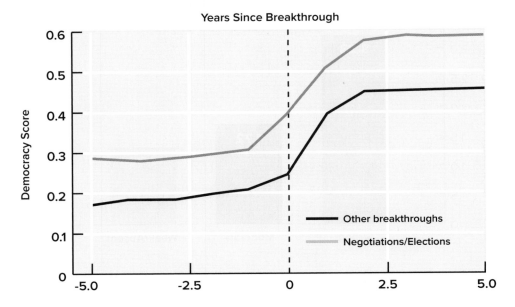

FIGURE 19: Average Levels of Democracy Across Different Breakthroughs

Source: Jonathan Pinckney, *How to Win Well: Civil Resistance Breakthroughs and the Path to Democracy* (Washington, DC: ICNC Press, 2021), 12.

A dashed vertical line indicates the breakthrough year. Democracy is measured using the Polyarchy score from the Varieties of Democracy project (Coppedge et al.2018), which ranges from 0 (not democratic at all) to 1 (completely democratic).

in the status of democracy. For example, assume the average free country has a score of 2, and the average not free country has a score of 6, the difference between free and not free is about 4 points.

Freedom House scores for strong coalition countries are 3.23 higher (on the 7-point scale) at the end versus the beginning of a nonviolent conflict, representing a massive jump in the state of democracy—almost the entire journey from not free to free. Scores for weak coalition countries saw only an increase of 1.32. The greater the strength of the coalition during the nonviolent conflict, the more democratic the post-conflict society will be. Today, if every country which is on balance not free were to experience this 3.23 jump in ranking, the world's most dangerous threats to world order and peace would melt away.

As a tyrant loses legitimacy, the discussions among pro-democracy activists and the citizens they represent—about the shape of the future democracy—should increase in frequency and specificity. A general recognition that the probability of victory is increasing means the civil resistance campaign should be able to tolerate more disagreement. A crucial leadership skill is to manage the timing of when and how these tensions are expressed as the transition to a new democratic order is ushered in.

One final risk factor that may derail a democratic outcome is when tyrants and their loyalists refuse to accept defeat. What is the prospect of a resurgence of the tyrant's fortunes that may create new fissures within the population and among dissidents?

To prevent this kind of late-stage reversal, some event is needed to mark the conflict's end. Pinckney has identified six "breakthrough" events enabling civil resistance campaigns to "move from the streets to the corridors of power... resulting in... a significant change in the incumbent regime."[49] They are:

- National negotiations between the opposition and the undemocratic regime
- Competitive national elections
- Resignation of the head of the undemocratic regime
- External interventions
- Coup d'état (violent or peaceful)
- Overwhelming the undemocratic regime[50]

Figure 19 shows that two breakthrough events in particular offer the best prospects for long-term democratic governance: national negotiations and competitive national elections.[51]

Pro-democracy activists should expect that the international community will continue to be helpful in fostering free and fair elections and negotiating for peace.[52]

---

49 Jonathan Pinckney, *How to Win Well: Civil Resistance Breakthroughs and the Path to Democracy* (Washington, DC: ICNC Press, 2021), 5.

50 This is the equivalent of Sharp's mechanism when the tyranny disintegrates.

51 Pinckney, *How to Win Well*, 13.

52 For further discussion of the role of the international community, please see the Declaration of Global Principles by the Global Network of Domestic Election Monitors (GNDEM) which has 251 member organizations in 89 countries and territories, and the recent paper "Mediating Mass Movements" by Maria Stephan, which discusses the value of outside negotiators in mediating the end of a nonviolent campaign. https://www.hdcentre.org/wp-content/uploads/2020/09/Mediating-Mass-Movements.pdf.

It is possible that the one million people living under the most tyrannical regimes will become significantly more aware of the possibilities of civil resistance. While this number may seem low compared to the billions of citizens on this planet, it is a frightening statistic for authoritarians, especially because this number can continue to rise rapidly.

Chapter Five

HOW DISSIDENTS INCREASE CONFIDENCE:

The Checklist Exercise for Freedom

The checklist questions described in the previous chapters, if utilized properly, can become an extraordinary training tool for dissidents. These questions provide the logical next step for graduates of civil resistance workshops, enabling them to scale the development of skills among fellow pro-democracy activists while remaining inside their own countries. But can the Checklist also be used by dissidents who have never before been to a workshop? The answer is yes, and this has significant implications for the future prospects of democracy in the world.

A traditional civil resistance workshop curriculum offers individual participants the most efficient forum to gain generalizable insights about nonviolent conflict. The eight checklist questions have the potential to develop group clarity and consensus about the best path forward to victory at any specific moment during a campaign of civil resistance. Most importantly, that path can be discovered by indigenous pro-democracy activists without the need to rely on the advice of so-called experts outside the country.

In the period between the completion of my doctorate and the publication of my first book, I spent fifteen years working on Wall Street. During most of this time I was head of capital markets for a prominent investment bank. It was a fascinating job that exposed me to talented executives from a wide variety of industries, including manufacturing, service, technology, food, healthcare, and media. I noticed they all had a common problem: how to take the best employees from various departments—product development, marketing, finance, human resources, and legal—and persuade them to commit to solving one another's problems.

A common approach was to convene an intimate retreat for one or two days that involved three steps. The first step was to create mutual awareness of one another's needs and limitations. The next step was to brainstorm the best opportunities for cooperative behavior. The final step was to commit to one another the execution of specific tasks that would lead to coordinated solutions in furtherance of the enterprise's mission.

Our firm went through a similar exercise. Our chief executive officer mandated that key members of the corporate finance and high yield departments convene for 36 hours. The purpose was to discover new ways to grow our investment banking revenue as quickly as possible. There was initial reluctance to waste time on abstract ideas instead of focusing on the specific transactions that needed immediate attention. However, after the 36 hours ended, everyone in the room recognized the value of what was jointly experienced. Over a ten-year period the firm went from ranking twenty-sixth in investment banking revenue to number one.

The Checklist Exercise for Freedom was designed to mirror the 36-hour session I experienced as a financier. Without relying on outside expertise I expect dissidents collaborating together over a similar short period of time will find ways to dramatically improve their competitive position versus their tyrannical adversaries. Building confident team cultures will create an insurmountable competitive advantage. Tyrants of the world beware when one million pro-democracy activists complete the exercise.

The point has been made often in this book that the tyrant's greatest asset is the disorientation of the population. What follows is an antidote: the Checklist Exercise for Freedom.

The Checklist Exercise has five phases:

- Organizational
- Introductory
- Assessment
- Innovation
- Commitment

■ ORGANIZATIONAL PHASE

The first phase involves preparation activities. These include appointing a facilitator (and perhaps an assistant), recruiting participants, and finding a suitable location to meet.

The primary duty of the facilitator is to ensure that each participant's ideas are fully and accurately communicated. It is helpful, though not mandatory, that the facilitator has a deep understanding of civil resistance. Obviously one source of facilitators would be people who have past exposure to civil resistance content, although not every dissident necessarily makes the best facilitator.

The facilitator is responsible for recruiting twenty people for a 36-hour session. It is optimal if the participants represent a widely diversified set of interests. The greater the likelihood of sharp disagreements, the better. Why? Because early frictions can evolve into higher levels of mutual understanding and trust. Incidents of transformation among participants are part of what makes the Checklist Exercise so powerful.

The facilitator must speak to all the participants ahead of time to get a sense of their background and perspective, and to establish trust. Of particular importance is to determine whether each participant has thoughtfully considered and appreciates the usefulness of the five messages listed in Chapter 2 (see Table 4 on page 24). The facilitator's role will include making sure disagreements do not sour the exercise. Knowing the motivations of each participant may become critical to constructively bring tensions to the surface, and also to help resolve them.

The next obligation of the facilitator is to find a place to convene in person. This may require seeking funding. First and foremost, the location needs to be shielded from outside interference. The location should be spacious enough to accommodate all the participants together as well as the need to deliberate individually in private. Also, over the 36 hours the participants need to have access to the necessary amenities to keep them focused completely on the task at hand.

The facilitator must also bring large easel pads and thick markers to transcribe what is said. As each sheet fills up with information it should be taped to the wall so each participant can keep track of other participants ideas. Finally, the facilitator needs to ensure that every participant has adequate supplies of paper and pens to perform their individual tasks.

■ INTRODUCTORY PHASE

The purpose of the introductory phase is to make participants comfortable regarding who else is in the room and why they are qualified to be there. It is also the moment to ensure each participant is clear about key concepts of civil resistance. The participants should—at minimum—read this book and absorb the five ideas dissidents need to know in Chapter 2.

This exercise will not achieve its potential if participants are not clear about the meaning of each checklist question. To achieve clarity during the introductory phase, it may be worthwhile to ask the participants to voice their doubts if they may think the Checklist is neither clear, comprehensive, nor realistic. Inviting the participants to offer criticism at this stage can actually help them better understand the meaning and purpose of each checklist question.

Active dialogue will allow the facilitator to clarify for participants questions of terminology (e.g., explaining that civil resistance is different than nonviolence) that can be a source of confusion in the assessment and innovation phases.

Finally, the facilitator will outline what is expected of the participants during the assessment, innovation, and commitment phases.

■ ASSESSMENT PHASE

The assessment phase begins with the facilitator asking each participant to find a secluded spot to analyze the Checklist from two perspectives in the following order:

- First, answer each of the checklist questions with a score between 1–10. A very strong "yes" would be a 10 and a very strong "no" would be a 1.

- Next, rank Checklist Questions 1–4 (Building Capabilities) in order of importance. A "1" would be the most important and a "4" would be the least important.

- Finally, rank Checklist Questions 5–8 (Navigating Conflict) in order of importance. A "1" would be the most important and a "4" would be the least important.

THE CHECKLIST
EXERCISE FOR FREEDOM

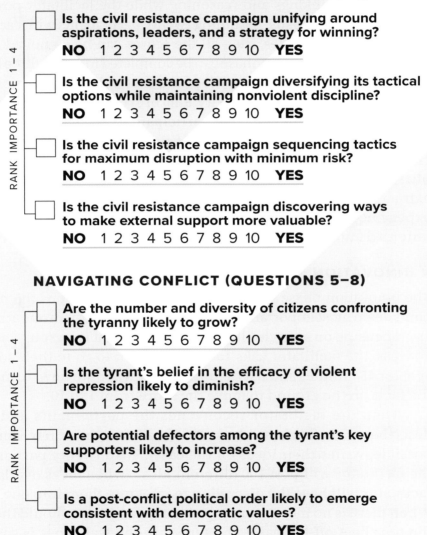

BUILDING CAPABILITIES (QUESTIONS 1–4)

RANK IMPORTANCE 1 – 4

☐ Is the civil resistance campaign unifying around aspirations, leaders, and a strategy for winning?
NO 1 2 3 4 5 6 7 8 9 10 **YES**

☐ Is the civil resistance campaign diversifying its tactical options while maintaining nonviolent discipline?
NO 1 2 3 4 5 6 7 8 9 10 **YES**

☐ Is the civil resistance campaign sequencing tactics for maximum disruption with minimum risk?
NO 1 2 3 4 5 6 7 8 9 10 **YES**

☐ Is the civil resistance campaign discovering ways to make external support more valuable?
NO 1 2 3 4 5 6 7 8 9 10 **YES**

NAVIGATING CONFLICT (QUESTIONS 5–8)

RANK IMPORTANCE 1 – 4

☐ Are the number and diversity of citizens confronting the tyranny likely to grow?
NO 1 2 3 4 5 6 7 8 9 10 **YES**

☐ Is the tyrant's belief in the efficacy of violent repression likely to diminish?
NO 1 2 3 4 5 6 7 8 9 10 **YES**

☐ Are potential defectors among the tyrant's key supporters likely to increase?
NO 1 2 3 4 5 6 7 8 9 10 **YES**

☐ Is a post-conflict political order likely to emerge consistent with democratic values?
NO 1 2 3 4 5 6 7 8 9 10 **YES**

It should not be assumed that the checklist questions with the strongest "no" are the most important for the group to address. Here is where the Checklist Exercise can be most relevant. While the checklist questions were formulated on the assumption that they are of equal significance, only local dissidents can accord them the proper priority for their circumstances.

The solitary analysis should be done in 45 minutes and then the facilitator should reconvene the entire group. Each person should present their rankings and reasoning while the facilitator posts the scores on the easel pads. Assuming twenty participants with each presenting for five minutes, then all the scores can be compiled in 100 minutes. The assessment phase can be completed in under three hours.

It is very important in each phase that individual participants advance their views with clarity and brevity. There should be no "heat seeking missiles" by one participant to shoot down the ideas of another. There will be plenty of time for rigorous debate and criticism during the breaks and meals and during the commitment phase. The purpose of the assessment and innovation phases are to extract the best ideas from every participant based on their unique experiences. Conformity of views is reaffirming only when it is unforced and spontaneous.

■ INNOVATION PHASE

The innovation phase focuses on the checklist questions the participants deem most important and is spent addressing them one at a time.

Focusing on a single checklist question that the group chose to address, the facilitator asks each participant to go to their solitary spot for 45 minutes and list their five best ideas as to how to improve the facts on the ground to move the score from 1 to 10.

Then the facilitator reconvenes the participants and each describes their five best ideas. The facilitator, in as few words as possible, writes their ideas on the easel. With twenty participants the facilitator will post 100 different ideas (when ideas overlap the facilitator will have the discretion to integrate them into one idea). When there is no more room to write, the facilitator should then rip the top sheet off the easel and tape it to the wall, so it is easy for everyone to see and refer to.

Then the facilitator asks each participant to go back to their solitary spot for 15 minutes, look at all of the ideas for improvement on the wall and pick the five best that are not their own. When they reconvene, the facilitator puts a check mark next to each of the participant's five choices not their own, creating 100 separate checkmarks. It is then possible for the facilitator to write down and rank on a separate easel pad the 10 ideas with the most checkmarks.

The innovation phase can be completed in under three hours.

■ COMMITMENT PHASE

At this point, tremendous buy-in from the participants is present as they witness and evaluate the different points of view of their colleagues regarding what it will take to beat their adversaries. The commitment phase is less structured and more subjective than the other phases. The previous phases should have given the group a sense of what it needs to do to triumph over the tyrant. The commitment phase seeks to answer the question: Who among us should take responsibility for specific steps to achieve this goal?

Finding answers to this question defines the purpose of the Checklist Exercise for Freedom. However, there are no right or wrong answers. There are only authentic answers based on indigenous participants' responses versus inauthentic answers from those outside the conflict and immune from the risks of a tyrant's repression.

Separating the authentic from the inauthentic requires facilitators to be disciplined in their role. They must refrain from offering their own tactical or strategic opinions and focus instead on encouraging the expression of what the participants consider their best ideas. If every idea is respected and then prioritized by the participants themselves, the result will be greater confidence to act.

The foundation for a successful commitment phase is laid in the first 24 hours. The half-hour breaks and meals allow the participants to ask each other questions and to explore areas of agreement and disagreement as well as their ideas about next steps for their civil resistance campaigns. The commitment phase will allow stored up energy and enthusiasm to be expressed based on ideas already tested among the participants.

The commitment phase does not need a solitary component. It is a group discussion that for the first time will include intense criticism and debate. The commitment phase ends when the participants are satisfied that they all have enough to do to move the momentum of the conflict in their direction.

TABLE 16: The 36-Hour Checklist Exercise Schedule	
DAY 1	
7:00 am – 8:00 am	Breakfast
8:00 am – 10:00 am	*Introductory Phase*
10:00 am – 10:30 am	Break
10:30 am – 1:00 pm	*Assessment Phase*
1:00 pm – 2:00 pm	Lunch
2:00 pm – 4:30 pm	*Innovation Phase* for the Key Checklist Question on Building Capabilities (45 minutes solitary, 1:45 minutes group)
4:30 pm – 5:00 pm	Break
5:00 pm – 5:45 pm	*Commitment Phase* for the Key Checklist Question on Building Capabilities (Session 1)
6:15 pm – 7:15 pm	Dinner
7:15 pm – 9:00 pm	*Commitment Phase* for the Key Checklist Question on Building Capabilities (Session 2)
DAY 2	
7:00 am – 8:00 am	Breakfast
8:00 am – 10:30 am	*Innovation Phase* for the Key Checklist Question on Navigating Conflict (45 minutes solitary, 1:45 minutes group)
10:30 am – 11:00 am	Break
11:00 am – 12:30 pm	*Commitment Phase* for the Key Checklist Question on Navigating Conflict (Session 1)
12:30 pm – 1:30 pm	Lunch
1:30 pm – 3:00 pm	*Commitment Phase* for the Key Checklist Question on Navigating Conflict (Session 2)
3:00 pm – 7:00 pm	Unstructured time (for example, the group might decide to work on Innovation and Commitment for other Checklist Questions)

A measure of success will be whether participants choose to reconvene a future Checklist Exercise among themselves after a period of months in order to review their progress. This will show that they understand that they have significant power to influence the course of their conflict. It will also show their determination to recommit to what needs to be done at that moment in time to maximize the prospect of winning. Checklist Exercises are a way to simultaneously confirm progress and respond to the changing realities for the nonviolent conflict. Having experienced the power of the assessment, innovation, and commitment phases they will be confident of the results of going through those phases again. They may even want to choose their own facilitator which would be an indicator that they would want to convene new groups on their own.

It is possible to scale dramatically the number of people exposed to civil resistance via the Checklist Exercise for Freedom. Imagine that the number of participants in offline and online workshops[53] grows to 2,500 people per year and that each of them learns how to facilitate a 36-hour Checklist Exercise for Freedom. If they commit to organizing five seminars per year with 20 participants each in their own country, it is possible that within four years one million people living under the most tyrannical regimes will become significantly more knowledgeable as to the potential of civil resistance. While this number may seem low in comparison to the billions of citizens on this planet, it is a frightening statistic for authoritarians, especially because this number can continue to rise rapidly over time.

> *Checklist Exercises are a way to simultaneously confirm progress and respond to the changing realities for the nonviolent conflict.*

This points to the passage of time as one of the most important advantages that campaigns of civil resistance have compared to violent insurgencies. Leaders of violent insurgencies must quickly reverse a regime's early military advantages. They accomplish this by killing as many as possible of the government's security forces and creating deserters among the others. However, if the government's military advantage is not quickly reversed, then the violent insurgency will quickly be exposed to superior violence that can destroy its viability.

By way of contrast, nonviolent movements can take their time. They can deescalate and then escalate and again deescalate their tactics of resistance. They can play a long-term game of attrition against a tyrant, reaping strategic gains even if their resistance

---

53 The best option for the Checklist Exercise, if circumstances permit, is to have an in-person meeting. This will foster sustained interest and depth of interaction among participants. However, if public health, financial limitations, or logistical or security challenges prevent an in-person meeting, people can try to organize the exercise virtually on an online conferencing platform if that is possible for them and communication can be secured. Which platform participants use and how they use it will depend on the usability and security implications of the country or countries in which participants are based.

seemingly retreats to private and family spaces before it publicly reemerges with force. Throughout this entire time, the authoritarian needs to stay alert, keeping his resources committed, which drives up the costs of trying to maintain his control.

One way to keep the battlefield fresh is to proliferate these checklist exercises.

Tyrants reading this book—and it can be expected that some of them will—should come to realize that a campaign of civil resistance can never be fully extinguished. No matter how dire the circumstances, citizens can always convene a Checklist Exercise for Freedom.

A tyrant sends his henchmen to seize armaments to counter a violent insurrection. But what does the tyrant's henchman seize when confronted with people doing a Checklist Exercise? Trying to break up these exercises may end up with the henchman wanting to participate as a defector instead.

The battle between dissident and tyrant will be determined by which side has the confidence to continue in the conflict. The Checklist Exercise for Freedom keeps the pro-democracy activists on the battlefield, allowing them to see that there are always opportunities to improve their position. Even in the face of the worst oppression, dissidents can build unity, diversify tactics, and interact with potential defectors. The Checklist Exercise proves to the tyrant that eventually he must surrender power. This is not only true for "benign" tyrants but for all tyrants.

Recently one of the world's most brutal leaders, Omar al-Bashir of Sudan, was forced from power through a civil resistance campaign. He is now in prison facing trial for crimes against humanity. According to Stephen Zunes, there was a substantial effort to share knowledge about civil resistance:

> For several years leading up to the revolution, a number of international organizations... led workshops for civil society groups on civic education, conflict resolution, and other issues which likely contributed to the empowerment of activists, though trainings specifically dealing with strategies and tactics of civil resistance were exclusively of Sudanese origin.

> One of the groups which played an important role in promoting nonviolent means of resistance was the Organisation for Nonviolence

and Development [ONAD].... For years, the organization offered workshops throughout the country on such issues as peacebuilding, gender, human rights, civic education, institutional development, good governance, conflict resolution, interfaith dialogue, and group process. Given the destruction of most civil society institutions under the 30-year dictatorship and the divide-and-rule tactics of the regime, such seemingly apolitical topics ended up having significant political implications. In addition to the trainings in these areas, ONAD also led workshops focusing directly on strategic nonviolent action and maintaining nonviolent discipline in the face of attacks and other provocations by security forces....

While it developed its own curricula, ONAD was influenced by training manuals from various European and Indian groups, including the Gandhian Institute, War Resisters' International, and Swedish Fellowship of Reconciliation. Also valuable were DVDs and other materials documenting civil resistance campaigns and lessons learnt for activists from American educational foundations like the International Center on Nonviolent Conflict and the Albert Einstein Institution. ONAD estimates that it trained at least 10,000 people directly and 50,000 indirectly through its training for trainers. The organization's emphasis on nonviolent action increased over time, with close to 70% of its trainings focused on direct challenges to the government and other oppressive institutions. [54]

What happened to al-Bashir, which was a total surprise to regional experts, is no fluke but is the result of educating pro-democracy activists in the power of civil resistance.

ICNC will post this book for free online and also translate it into many languages. Because we expect tyrannical regimes will seek to expunge it from online reading by its citizens, we will also distribute it in flexible paperback form. This book, one way or the other, will cross borders even if tyrants try to stop it and be available to everyone who wants to become a more effective pro-democracy activist. It cannot be easily interdicted, and once inside a country it can be copied and shared. At this moment, there exists an opportunity to multiply a thousandfold the number of pro-democracy activists exposed to the skills needed to win their nonviolent conflict.

---

54 Stephen Zunes, *Sudan's 2019 Revolution: The Power of Civil Resistance* (Washington, DC: ICNC Press, 2021), 14–15.

At this very moment tyrants may be underestimating the risks that nonviolent conflict poses to them. This complacency creates vulnerabilities that can threaten the viability of even the most entrenched regimes including Iran, Russia, China, North Korea, Venezuela, and Myanmar.

Chapter Six

AN HISTORIC CHOICE:

Acquiescing to Tyranny or Igniting the Fourth Democratic Wave

The fate of billions of people around the world will be determined by the outcome of conflicts between dissidents and tyrants. It is estimated that 2.5 billion people in the world live under the scourge of tyranny. The lives of innocent citizens are dominated by the whims of unaccountable rulers who don't care about fundamental human rights. The consequences of this fact are immense. Many of the worst human acts in history have been perpetrated by tyrannies that have emerged from the oppression and depravity that tyrants create.

Tyrannies have changed their appearance over time, but their underlying dynamics and behaviors remain the same. Colonial empires looked different than Cold War dictatorships, which in turn look different than today's modern authoritarians who depend on technology. While this distinction can be important, it should not distract us from the prevailing realities of tyranny regardless of how it presents itself to the world. Whether a tyranny seems to outsiders as tech-savvy, isolationist, and unpredictable; theocratic; paternalistic; ideologically left or right, or any combination in between, we can identify it by the hardships that it creates for the people who live under it. Domestically, tyrannical regimes create societies in which:

- Fear is pervasive
- Corruption and manifestly unfair policies lead to massive stratification between wealth and extreme poverty

- Workers are exploited without recourse
- Humanitarian and public health crises are much more likely to emerge due to incompetence or deliberate indifference of powerholders
- Individuals can have their assets seized on a whim
- Elections are unfair, fraudulent, or nonexistent
- The judicial system is openly biased and serves the interests of elites, while individuals are subject to arbitrary detention
- The media and educational environment are monopolized by propaganda and disinformation
- Attempts to challenge or change the system by those who live under it are met with severe repression and systematic human rights abuse

While tyrannies are the primary cause of vast human suffering for domestic populations, their existence also has negative global consequences. Non-democratic governments heighten the incidence of war (both civil and inter-state), resulting in atrocities, extremism, humanitarian crises, human rights abuses, mass migration of refugees, and corruption (which often crosses borders). These authoritarian regimes increase state fragility and destroy sources of societal resilience. They further seek to undermine existing democracies and erode international law and institutions. They aim to pervert, through their membership, the mission of the Human Rights Council at the United Nations. A more authoritarian world is an unstable and dangerous world from which no country is immune.

In the continuing competition for power between tyrants and pro-democracy activists there have been long cycles of winners and losers. This explains why—since the early nineteenth century—democracy has progressed in a series of three waves. According to Samuel P. Huntington:

> The first "long" wave of democratization began in the 1820s, with the widening of the suffrage to a large proportion of the male population in the United States, and continued for almost a century... until 1926, bringing into being some 29 democracies. In 1922, however, the coming to power of Mussolini in Italy marked the beginning of a first 'reverse wave' that by 1942 had reduced the number of democratic states in the world to 12. The triumph of the Allies in

World War II initiated a second wave of democratization that reached its zenith in 1962 with 36 countries governed democratically, only to be followed by a second reverse wave (1960-1975) that brought the number of democracies back down to 30.[55]

The Third Democratic Wave began in 1974 with the Carnation Revolution in Portugal. It then migrated to countries in Latin America, Asia Pacific, Eastern Europe, and Sub-Saharan Africa. According to the Freedom House rankings, 35 countries during this approximate period (1972–2005) went from a ranking of "not free" or "partly free" to "free."[56] The most significant feature of the Third Democratic Wave was how the overwhelming majority of these transitions to freedom occurred via nonviolent campaigns of civil resistance.

The last half of the Third Wave was met with great optimism. Its spirit was codified in Francis Fukuyama's seminal work, *The End of History and the Last Man,* published in 1992 just after the end of the Cold War, as the Third Wave was gathering additional momentum. Fukuyama's central argument was that human political organizing has a final destination or equilibrium point for all mankind which is Western liberal democracy.

All political communities must make use of the desire for recognition, while at the same time protecting themselves from its destructive effects. If contemporary constitutional government has indeed found a formula whereby all are recognized in a way that nonetheless avoids the emergence of tyranny, then it would indeed have a special claim to stability and longevity among the regimes that have emerged on earth.[57]

Unfortunately, since 2005, Freedom House has recorded fifteen straight years of declining aggregate world rankings. As the Third Democratic Wave recedes from memory, the growth of authoritarian rule and its handmaiden, which is corrupt governance, may seem unstoppable. Not surprisingly, Fukuyama's thesis is now wrongly held in derision as the brand name for naivety.

The question today is, will the counter-wave we are now in be followed by a Fourth Democratic Wave? If this occurs Fukuyama's central thesis will ultimately be proven correct.

---

55 Samuel P. Huntington, "Democracy's Third Wave," in *Journal of Democracy* 2, no. 2 (1991): 1.

56 Karatnycky and Ackerman, 18.

57 Francis Fukuyama, *The End of History and the Last Man* (New York, NY: Free Press, 2006), xxi–xxii.

Realists reject the possibility of a Fourth Democratic Wave, believing that tyranny will remain a dominant force in world affairs. They think that now that the Third Democratic Wave has passed, civil resistance campaigns no longer threaten authoritarian rulers and cannot compete against the power of the state.

Tyrants once caught napping against the numerous civil resistance campaigns during the Third Democratic Wave are now collaborating with one other as to the best means of suppressing them. They are now more adept at consolidating power with little overt violence and at retaining power by judiciously threatening and using minimal levels of violence. New uses of technology for surveillance and tracking provide very important defenses against civil resistance, while also undermining institutions that protect political and human rights. Authoritarians feel they can act with greater impunity by ending term limits through legislative fiat, by shutting down media outlets that were the most vocal in support of everyone's political rights and civil liberties, and by more aggressive jailing or killing of pro-democracy activists.

Realists argue that the key reason why authoritarianism is now ascendant is because the United States—the flag-bearer of the "freedom" message—is no longer the sole superpower. Instead, the United States is in multi-dimensional competition between China, Russia, Iran, North Korea, and other hostile dictatorships. Without the prestige of American backing, the democracy promotion community that did such remarkable work after the Berlin Wall fell is now in full retreat.

> *The conceit that the United States can turn all countries into consolidated democracies has been disproved over and over again, from Vietnam to Afghanistan to Iraq. The view that Washington should offer a shining example but nothing more fails to appreciate the dangers of the contemporary world, in which groups and individuals with few resources can kill thousands or even hundreds of thousands of Americans. The United States cannot fix the world's problems, but nor does it have the luxury of ignoring them.* [58]

---

58 Stephen Krasner, "Learning to Live with Despots: The Limits of Democracy Promotion" *Foreign Affairs* 99, no. 2, (February 10, 2020). https://www.foreignaffairs.com/articles/2020-02-10/learning-live-despots.

The realist perspective is ingrained in almost all regional specialists whose primary focus is to explain the behavior of elites. They have difficulty according significance to developments at the grassroots level particularly with respect to changes in a tyrant's capacity to defend against nonviolent conflict. This explains why realists and regional specialists have an abysmal record in predicting when a civil resistance campaign is likely to begin. They are always surprised and tend to view mass protests, strikes, and boycotts as flukes that will soon end with no consequence.

Regional experts believed Serbian dictator Slobodan Milosevic would never leave office without first resorting to violence. The Green Movement in Iran was considered unthinkable until it occurred. Just prior to the 2011 uprising and occupation of Tahrir Square, regional specialists were certain the events in Tunisia would never spread to Egypt. And in Sudan it seemed fanciful that Omar al-Bashir could be removed from power and thrown in jail.

Realists and regional specialists have an abysmal record in predicting when a civil resistance campaign is likely to begin.

Realists do not differentiate between the fallout from failed violent insurrections and failed nonviolent insurrections. A violent insurrection is crushed when it encounters superior force from the tyrant's police and military. Those violent insurrectionists spared from execution or jail no longer have a cohesive force to resume the battle for years to come, if ever. However, a tyrant can never fully extinguish a failed civil resistance campaign. Even when tyrants prevail, they still must accommodate their citizens' basic necessities or they will lose the benefit of their apathy. This accommodation allows for even moribund civil resistance campaigns to resuscitate and lead to democracy years later.

During the last fifteen years of democratic backsliding, realists have pointed to the so-called demise of the Arab Spring as proof that advancement of democracy will be limited in the future. Others, however, view the Arab Uprisings as having never ended:

In 2021, there may be few beliefs more universally shared than that the Arab uprisings failed. It is easy to understand the appeal of this idea, eagerly promoted by autocratic regimes and foreign policy realists alike. It means a return to business as usual. Both the Obama and the Trump administrations tacitly accepted that view as they shifted their gaze to other goals in the region—the former to nuclear negotiations with Iran, the latter to normalizing Arab relations with Israel. Yet that conviction is in fact just the latest in a series of premature conclusions. Despite the Arab uprising's premature obituary and dark legacy, the revolutionary wave of 2011 was not a passing mirage. Ten years on, the region's autocratic façade is cracking once again. Major uprisings recently blocked the reelection of Algeria's infirm president, led to the overthrow of Sudan's long-ruling leader, and challenged sectarian political orders in Iraq and Lebanon. Lebanon barely has a government after a year of protests, financial disaster, and the fallout of an incomprehensible explosion at Beirut's port. Saudi Arabia has witnessed rapid change at home as it prepares for MBS's presumed royal ascension. [59]

Tyrants never feel they have enough power to be secure. They are the poster children for Lord Acton's infamous dictum, "Power tends to corrupt, and absolute power corrupts absolutely." The more they impose suffocating control on the populations they rule, the more likely it is that latent double thinkers will proliferate and over time transform into revealed double thinkers, and ultimately, defectors. This explains why even with the overall reduction in world freedom, the number of people power campaigns is growing at a record pace.

At this very moment tyrants may be underestimating the risks that nonviolent conflict poses to them. This complacency creates vulnerabilities that can threaten the viability of even the most entrenched regimes including Iran, Russia, China, North Korea, Venezuela, and Myanmar.

To prepare for the presentation of the Checklist Questions, in Chapter 2 I listed five ideas that dissidents must know first. However, there is a sixth idea for dissidents that is the most hopeful one of all (and which will become clearer as pro-democracy activists have gone through the Checklist Exercise for Freedom): While a dictator can destroy a guerrilla force and end a violent insurrection for decades if not forever, dictators can never really end a civil resistance campaign in support of democracy and human rights. One of the most encouraging pieces of research data is Figure 20, which shows that even a nonviolent conflict that has failed to achieve its goal still has a 35 percent chance of doing so in the next five years.

---

59   Marc Lynch, "The Arab Uprisings Never Ended: The Enduring Struggle to Remake the Middle East," in *Foreign Affairs* (January/February 2021).

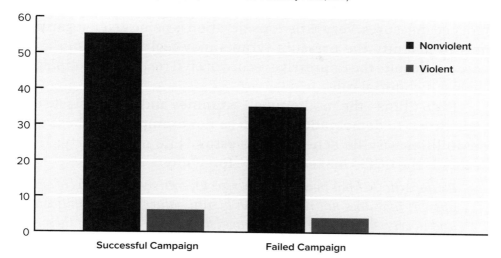

FIGURE 20: Probability That a Country Will Be a Democracy Five Years After a Campaign Ends

Source: Erica Chenoweth and Maria J. Stephan, *Why Civil Resistance Works: The Strategic Logic of Nonviolent Resistance* (New York, NY: Columbia University Press, 2011).

What then has been missing? In "The Future of Nonviolent Resistance," Erica Chenoweth provides evidence that shows that the skill levels of pro-democracy activists are declining. This includes:

- Public participation rates in civil resistance campaigns have dropped from 2.7 percent in the 1990s to 1.3 percent today.

- There is an overreliance on mass demonstrations versus other tactics with different risk profiles such as strikes and boycotts.

- There is an overreliance on the spontaneity of digital organizing instead of planning crucial tactical sequences.

- There is an increased willingness to indirectly associate with violent actors in the belief this will increase chances of success.[60]

As campaigns of nonviolent conflict increase, it is inevitable that without a proportional expansion of training, the probability of improving success rates will decline. Now imagine what would happen if increases in the number of campaigns were matched by increases in the numbers of dissidents who have completed the Checklist Exercise for Freedom. This is what will be required to ignite the Fourth Democratic Wave.

As of this writing, great power conflicts are intensifying between the United States and its democratic (and certain undemocratic)

---

60 Chenoweth, "The Future of Nonviolent Resistance."

allies versus China, Russia, and Iran. In a US-led alliance, media pundits, think tank professionals, and government policymakers are focused nearly exclusively on pressuring authoritarians with sanctions, military buildups, and alliance building—all externally induced measures. Very little consideration is being given regarding how to magnify the pressure tyrants may feel from *within* their borders, despite the impressive record of civil resistance campaigns against dictatorial rule.

Even China—the mother of all tyrannies and the greatest strategic threat to democratic nations—is not exempt from these vulnerabilities. Orville Schell, in his essay "Life of the Party: How Secure Is the CCP?," makes this case forcefully:

> *Perhaps the CCP has managed to perfect an entirely new model of development that does not require such quaint values as freedom, justice, and liberty. But modern history suggests that the absence of these elements can imperil a country. Think of fascist Italy and Germany, imperial Japan, Francoist Spain, theocratic Iran, and the Soviet Union.*
>
> *....Might the Chinese just be different from everyone else, especially those in the West? Perhaps, some say, Chinese citizens will prove content to gain wealth and power alone, without these aspects of life that other societies have commonly considered fundamental to being human. Such an assumption seems unrealistic, not to say patronizing. In the end, the Chinese people will likely prove little different in their yearnings from Canadians, Czechs, Japanese, or Koreans. Just because those outside China cannot see or hear a more fulsome expression of universal values right now does not mean that such desires do not exist. Stilled for the moment, they have appeared again and again in the past and are bound to reappear in the future.*[61]

Leaders past and present, policy analysts, and media from the world's oldest democracies need to study civil resistance with fresh eyes. They need to abandon widely held beliefs that civil resistance must fail, or worse, be pointless during conflicts with one or more violent protagonists. There is no context where realists are more certain that civil resistance cannot initiate a democratic transition than in civil wars. The reasoning is that at the conclusion of such

---

61 Orville Schell, "Life of the Party: How Secure Is the CCP?" *Foreign Affairs* (July/August 2021): 74–75.

intensely violent conflicts, the winner will certainly impose a cruel dictatorship over the loser. However, Luke Abbs, having analyzed nearly six decades of data on the impact of nonviolent resistance in civil wars, presents an unexpected finding:

Figure 21 visualizes the likelihood of civil war "surviving" on the y-axis and the number of civil war episodes' years on the x-axis. At all stages of the lifecycle in all civil wars in the data, the likelihood of the violent conflict continuing is substantially reduced when largescale nonviolent campaigns are present within the conflict. For instance, after 5 years of civil war, a peace agreement is around 25 percent more likely when nonviolent campaigns are present compared to when they are not.[62]

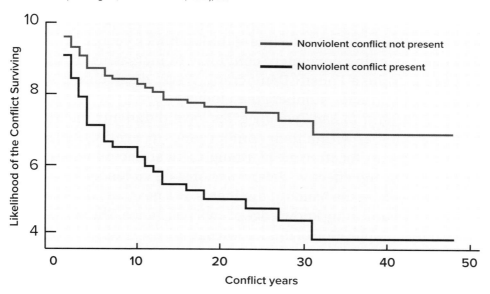

FIGURE 21: Nonviolent Campaigns and the Duration of Civil War (1955–2013)

Source: Luke Abbs, *The Impact of Nonviolent Resistance on the Peaceful Transformation of Civil War* (Washington, DC: ICNC Press, 2021), 33.

The policy opportunity is to identify how outsiders can help nurture nonviolent movements, which are already arising organically. In their research, *The Role of External Support in Nonviolent Campaigns*, Chenoweth and Stephan's most salient finding was that "training support is consistently impactful":

---

62 Abbs, *The Impact of Nonviolent Resistance*, 38.

Training is the only form of assistance that is positively correlated with nonviolent campaign characteristics. This is particularly true during the pre-campaign period, where higher incidence of training is correlated with higher participation rates, lower campaign fatalities, and higher probabilities of security force defections once the campaign has mobilized. Training during the campaign's peak mobilization is also correlated with an increase in participation size and with the ultimate success of the campaign. Across all models, training appears to have no systematic, observed downsides—and it is the only form of support with consistently positive correlations across all models. [63]

Larry Diamond, the preeminent scholar on democracy, observes:

The world is now immersed in a fierce global contest of ideas, information, and norms. In the digital age, that contest is moving at lightning speed on an hourly basis, and it is shaping how people think about their political systems and the future world order. Now especially—when doubts and threats to democracy are mounting in the West—this is not a contest that the democracies can afford to lose. [64]

Reversing the democratic decline of the last fifteen years will require dissidents winning nonviolent conflict with increasing frequency. If there is to be a Fourth Democratic Wave, dissidents must be trained in far greater numbers than today.

The Checklist to End Tyranny gives local dissidents the tools to train one another within their conflict zones, providing them with "greater capacity for strategic planning, tactical discipline, resource mobilization, and effective deterrence of state violence."[65]

This book, in the hands of dissidents, is a next step in the evolution of communicating knowledge of civil resistance. The availability and strategic application of this knowledge in every future nonviolent conflict can radically shift the balance of power away from the tyrant and back to pro-democracy activists where it belongs.

---

63   Chenoweth and Stephan, *The Role of External Support*, 65–66.

64   Larry Diamond, "America's Silence Helps Autocrats Triumph," *Foreign Policy,* September 6, 2019, https://foreignpolicy.com/2019/09/06/americas-silence-helps-autocrats-triumph-democratic-rollback-recession-larry-diamond-ill-winds/# .

65   Chenoweth and Stephan, *The Role of External Support*, 67.

At right: Lech Walesa, leader of Solidarity, celebrates the establishment of the farmers' union in Poland, 1981.

Above: Mkhuseli Jack leads the Port Elizabeth consumer boycott against apartheid, South Africa, 1985.

Left: Posters used to rally support for the boycott.

Appendix

Workshop and Online Course Evaluations

Over time, ICNC has received a great deal of feedback on our work and engagement around the world. In response to specific requests, we have held many seminars and workshops, and we have also organized recurring annual educational programs. These recurring programs include:

Summer Institutes: From 2006 to 2016, ICNC partnered with the Fletcher School of Law and Diplomacy to offer 5- and 6-day workshops on civil resistance to people from around the world. See a sample Summer Institute agenda in Table 17 on page 137.

Regional Institutes: In February 2018, ICNC collaborated with several local partners to establish a regional institute for the study of nonviolent conflict in Quito, Ecuador. Thirty-five participants from eleven countries in and around South America attended a six-day seminar that year. In the fall of 2018, a second institute was collaboratively organized and held in Kyiv, Ukraine, focusing on Eastern Europe and Central Asia and attracting forty participants from ten countries. A third institute was organized with local partners in Kathmandu, Nepal, partnering with local universities and NGOs to share research, civil resistance strategies, and movement experiences with dissidents and pro-democracy activists, and attracting thirty-six participants from twelve countries.

Online Courses: ICNC began running its flagship online course in 2012, in conjunction with Rutgers University.[66] "People Power: The Strategic Dynamics of Civil Resistance" attracts participants from countries around the world for a 7-week intensive, covering the following topics:

MODULE 1. Introduction to the Course: Welcome and Orientation Webinars • Participant Introductions • Present Knowledge Survey

---

66 In 2020, ICNC started to run the course without Rutgers University.

MODULE 2. Foundation of Civil Resistance: What Is Civil Resistance? • The Effectiveness of Civil Resistance

MODULE 3. Cases of Civil Resistance Around the World: National Liberation Cases • Civil Safety and Autonomy Cases • Defense and Expansion of Rights Cases • Public Accountability Cases

MODULE 4. Strategies and Tactics of Civil Resistance: Analyzing Nashville Lunch Counter Campaign • The Role of Women in Civil Resistance • Strategic Planning and Tactical Choices • Conflict Analysis Tools

MODULE 5. Repression, Backfire, and Defections: Repression and Backfire • Movement Strategies for Defections

MODULE 6. Violent Flanks, Agents Provocateurs, and Maintaining Nonviolent Discipline: Violent Flanks • An Inoculation Guide Against Agents Provocateurs • Maintaining Nonviolent Discipline

MODULE 7. New Frontiers in Civil Resistance Studies: Democratization and Civil Resistance • Civil Resistance Against Abusive Corporate Practices • Civil Resistance and Faith Communities • Cultural Resistance

MODULE 8. Completing the Course: Learning Gains Survey • Course Evaluations

Going beyond written and verbal feedback, our quantitative data reinforces what we've been told by ICNC program alumni, grantees, and collaborators. For example, below are the 2018 evaluation results for ICNC's 7-week online course "People Power: The Strategic Dynamics of Civil Resistance," which engages 55 to 65 people from around the world per year. To evaluate this course, ICNC conducted:

- An immediate pre-course assessment to discern participant knowledge, attitudes, and activities

- An immediate post-course assessment to discern participant knowledge, attitudes, and activities, so that changes as a result of the course can be ascertained

- An overall course evaluation in which participants give feedback on the course itself

TABLE 17: Sample Summer Institute Agenda

Session	Monday	Tuesday	Wednesday	Thursday	Friday
9:00–10:30	Introductions of All Participants and Faculty for the Week	Nonviolent Discipline and Violent Flanks *Exercise – Activity optional*	Repression and Backfire *Exercise – Activity optional*	Language and Meaning in Movements	Civilian Agency in Disrupted Societies and/or Countering Violent Non-State Actors
10:30–11:00	Break				
11:00–12:30	Introduction to Civil Resistance	Why Civil Resistance Movements Fail?	External Actors and Civil Resistance Movements	Nonviolent Defense against External Aggression	Campaigns against Corruption
12:30–2:00	Lunch	Lunch Speaker: Peter Ackerman	James Lawson Award Luncheon	Lunch **Breakout Session 2:**	Group photo Lunch
2:00–3:30	Movement Emergence and Sustainability *Exercise – Activity optional*	Panel: Gender and Civil Resistance		Civil Resistance Strategies for Peacebuilding and Transitional Justice Civil Resistance against Unjust Corporate Actors Break	Consolidating Gains and Democratic Transitions
3:30–4:00	Break	Break	Break	**Breakout Session 3:** Countering Violent Extremism Diasporas and Civil Resistance Violent Extremism Digital Resistance	Break
4:00–5:30	Strategy and Tactics *Exercise – Activity optional*	**Breakout Session 1:** How and Why Civil Resistance Movements Cause Defections? Arts and Cultural Resistance Civil Resistance and International Human Rights	**Breakout Groups** Exercise and Mid-week Evaluation	**Breakout Session 4:** Teaching, Sharing, and Translating Knowledge about Civil Resistance Media Coverage for Movement Success	Continuing Engagement and Final Evaluations
5:30–7:00	Dinner	Dinner	Charles River Cruise	Dinner	Free Time
7:00–9:00	"Ignite" Presentations Stories of Civil Resistance	Special Guest Presentations	Charles River Cruise	Free Evening	Graduation Ceremony and Dinner

- A three-month post-course assessment, so that we can determine how knowledge from the course has influenced participants' subsequent choices and actions

Here are some key findings from our 2018 three-month post-course assessment:

I. Respondents reported significant gains in effectiveness at planning and engaging in civil resistance.

- 94 percent reported that *their skills at planning civil resistance campaigns had improved* after taking ICNC's course.
- 94 percent said that they *were more effective in achieving their goals in civil resistance campaigns or trainings* after taking ICNC's course, with 62 percent reporting that they were "much more" (5 on a scale of 5) or significantly more (4 on a scale of 5) effective.
- 94 percent said that they *were more effective in writing, teaching, or researching about civil resistance* after taking ICNC's course, with 75 percent reporting that they were "much more" (5 on a scale of 5) or significantly more (4 on a scale of 5) effective.
- 86 percent reported that *the civil resistance actions in which they participated after ICNC's course were more effective than before the course*, with 50 percent reporting that the civil resistance actions in which they participated were "much more" (5 on a scale of 5) or significantly more (4 on a scale of 5) effective.

II. Respondents reported greater involvement in civil resistance campaigns, as well as writing, teaching, and researching about civil resistance.

- 56 percent of respondents said that *ICNC's course was very influential on their subsequent decision to join a civil resistance campaign.*
- 62 percent of respondents said that *they became more active in leading or planning a civil resistance campaign* after taking ICNC's course.
- 62 percent of respondents said that *they became more active in writing, teaching and researching about civil resistance* after taking ICNC's course.

III. Respondents reported that they were directly applying knowledge introduced in the course and referring back to it after the course.

Immediately after the course:

- 75 percent of respondents said that they had applied knowledge from the course in *planning civil resistance campaigns.*

- 75 percent of respondents said that they had applied knowledge from the course in *training or teaching about civil resistance.*

- 62 percent of respondents said that they had applied knowledge from the course in *writing about civil resistance.*

- 56 percent of respondents said that they had applied knowledge from the course when engaging directly in nonviolent actions.

Three months after the course:

- 100 percent of respondents said that *they had returned to ICNC's e-classroom to refer back to course materials* at least 1–5 times since the course ended, with 50 percent reporting that they had done so 6–10 times, and 6 percent reporting that they had done so 11–15 times.

- Six strategic planning tools were introduced during the course. After the course, no fewer than 56 percent of respondents said that *they were applying each of these tools more often than before the course,* and three planning tools were reported to be used more often by 69 percent of respondents.

IV. Respondents reported that they were more interested in learning about civil resistance after the course, and a significant number reported that three months after the course, they found the course content even more valuable than immediately after the course.

- 94 percent said that after the course, *they were more interested in learning about civil resistance.*

- 44 percent of respondents said that three months after ICNC's course ended, *they found the course content even more valuable than immediately after the course had ended.*

V. Respondents (who come from countries all over the world) reported that they kept in touch with each other after the course.

- 44 percent of respondents said that *they had communicated with at least one other course participant about civil resistance* 1–5 times since the course ended.

- 12 percent reported 6–10 communications since the course ended.

- 19 percent reported over 21 communications since the course ended.

These findings are confirmed by other quantitative evaluation data that ICNC has received. For example, the immediate evaluation and the one-year post evaluation of ICNC's 2018 week-long regional institute on civil resistance in Quito, Ecuador, show similar results.[67] See key program outcomes[68]:

TABLE 18: Key Program Outcomes	
Increased knowledge	Peacebuilding concepts, theories, and cases that allow participants to socialize into the field, engage with other practitioners, and design better-informed interventions that reflect current best practices and well-developed theories of change.
Personal capacity building and professional development	Results in participants becoming more skilled at key tasks or having a more competitive profile for jobs, grants, academic programs.
Attitude changes, inspiration, and motivation	Encourages participants to continue in the field or to invest time/resources in peacebuilding work.
New projects	May include nongovernmental organizations, campaigns, replication trainings, and so on that build peace amongst a broader community that did not participate in the original training themselves, aided by technical assistance provided within the original training program (i.e., project incubators).
Greater social capital	Access to alumni networks or sponsoring organization portals that a. increase awareness/access to opportunities and resources that make subsequent actions possible, b. allow scaling up smaller initiatives by collaborating with people in other localities or issue areas, and c. disseminate information.
Amplified voices	Published articles, interviews, and newsletter spotlights bring greater visibility to the peacebuilding work of participants and provide a larger audience that they can reach to tell their own story of change (rather than having these stories filtered through donor reports or other mediated dissemination channels).

---

67 Some of these results were also published in peer-reviewed academic journals. See Jeffrey Pugh, "A Catalyst for Action: Training and Education as Networking Platforms for Peace Projects," *Journal of Peacebuilding & Development* 15, no. 1 (April 2020): 127–132; Jeffrey Pugh, "Weaving Transnational Activist Networks: Balancing International and Bottom-up Capacity-building Strategies for Nonviolent Action in Latin America," Middle Atlantic Review of Latin American Studies 2, no. 1 (June 2018): 130–144.

68 Pugh, "A Catalyst for Action," 130.

List of Tables

List of Figures

Photo Credits

Aside from the image of the author and Gene Sharp in Lithuania, all photographs are of successful civil resistance campaigns.

COVER: **Lana Haroun.**

PAGE ii: **Fethi Belaid/AFP via Getty Images.**

PAGE iv: **Cindy Karp/The Chronicle Collection via Getty Images.**

PAGE 12:   **Photograph provided by ICNC.**

PAGE 17:   **Sergei Supinsky/AFP via Getty Images.**

PAGE 38:   **Bettmann via Getty Images.**

PAGE 73:   **Peter Charlesworth/LightRocket via Getty Images.**

PAGE 105:   **Universal History Archive/Universal Images Group via Getty Images.**

PAGE 133:   **Bettman via Getty Images.**

PAGE 134:   **Photograph: Elijah Jokazi via Evening Post/ The Herald/Tisoblackstar.**

PAGE 144:   **Braca Nadezdic/Hulton Archive via Getty Images.**

Following page: Otpor uniting opposition against Slobodan Milosevic, Serbia, 2000.